ART MATTERS

John Tusa has been Managing Director of London's Barbican Centre since November 1995, during which time he has been repeatedly called upon to make a case for the arts to both government and funding.

After taking a First Class Honours Degree in History at Trinity College, Cambridge, he joined the BBC in 1960. During his subsequent career in broadcasting he was an award-winning presenter of BBC2's *Newsnight* (1980–1986) and then Managing Director of the BBC World Service (1986–1992).

He has written two collections of essays on broadcasting – *Conversations with the World* and *A World in Your Ear* – and with his wife, the historian Ann Tusa, collaborated on two books on contemporary history: *The Nuremberg Trial* and *The Berlin Airlift*. He has written and presented ten programmes in BBC Radio 4's survey of the twentieth century to mark the millennium: *Twenty-Twenty – A View of the Century*.

ART MATTERS

Reflecting on Culture

John Tusa

To Mave

Best wishes

John Tusa, April 2013.

Methuen

Published by Methuen 2000

3 5 7 9 10 8 6 4 2

First published in hardback in the United Kingdom in 1999 by
Methuen Publishing Limited
This paperback edition, with revisions, first published in the United Kingdom
in 2000 by Methuen Publishing Limited
215 Vauxhall Bridge Road, London SW1V 1EJ

Methuen Publishing Limited Reg. No. 3543167

A CIP catalogue record for this book
is available from the British Library

ISBN 0 413 75060 4

Typeset by Deltatype Ltd, Birkenhead, Merseyside
Printed and bound in Great Britain by
Creative Print and Design (Wales), Ebbw Vale

Papers used by Methuen Publishing Limited are natural,
recyclable products made from wood grown in sustainable forests.
The manufacturing processes conform to environmental
regulations of the country of origin.

Contents

Introduction

An article I had written expressing doubts about the direction and sense of purpose behind Labour's arts policy – 'I'm Worried about Tony' – appeared in *The Times* on 11 March 1998. By the time I got into the office that morning, there was a note from Michael Earley at Methuen suggesting that we should meet to discuss a collection of essays on the state of the arts in Britain today. This volume is the result.

A great deal of it had already been written, in the form of speeches or lectures given since becoming Managing Director of the Barbican Centre in November 1995. Other possible chapters were already in the pipeline in the form of booked speaking engagements. Between us, Michael Earley and I rejected some and decided on others that I would write up specially for the book. Finally, when the chosen essays had been identified, it was Michael who grouped them into three sections – Beliefs, Politics, Actions – having perceived a grouping of themes which I might have sensed but had not pinpointed so clearly. It was he who found the book its title. I am grateful to him for his wholehearted commitment to the project and his sharp and enthusiastic understanding of the issues discussed in it.

I am grateful too to the various institutions which provided the opportunity to set out my thoughts about these arts issues. They include the Anglo-Israeli Association ('A New Rhetoric for the Arts'); Battersea Arts Centre ('The Agony and the Ecstasy'); the British Council in Prague ('Culture and Identity'); the University of Portsmouth ('Is there Space for Art?'); the London School of Economics ('The Good Society'); the Marketing Association ('Art for Art's Sake'); Amsterdam Leisure and

Arts Consulting Group ('Marketing and the Arts'); and the Arts Administration School of City University ('The ABC of Running an Arts Centre'), our immediate neighbours at the Barbican, and where I am Visiting Professor.

The main problem with a collection such as this is that speeches and lectures have their own styles of writing. And since there is no logical rhyme or reason behind the invitations that one receives to speak, the same or similar subjects tend to reappear. To the extent that these chapters have been purged of the worst of their stylistic excesses of speech, and to the extent that repetitions have been reduced, though not wholly elimina-ted, I owe it to my wife, Ann Tusa. She brought her historian's eye – and the habits of a teacher – to the task of rigorous sub-editing and judicious rewriting of these chapters. I am grateful for the time and effort she devoted to them. In the end, an editor can only do as well as the material put into her hands.

A word on the second section, Politics. Some may think it rash for anyone involved in the day-to-day life of the British arts scene to appear to cross swords with its three leaders – the Prime Minister, the Culture Secretary and the Chairman of the Arts Council. My own view is that the questions of arts policy today are so important that everyone has a duty to become involved in that debate, and I have tried to address the issues and avoid the personalities. Both Chris Smith and Gerry Robinson set out their philosophies of arts funding and support in a substantial way. It is essential that those assumptions should be carefully scrutinised. That is all that I have tried to do.

Much of what I have written has been informed by my three and a half years as Managing Director of the Barbican Centre. During that time I have had unfailing support from my two Chairmen of the Barbican Centre Committee – first Geoffrey Lawson and, for the last two and a half years, Mrs Joyce Nash – and clear advice and strong backing from my immediate predecessor as Managing Director, the Town Clerk and Cham-berlain of the Corporation of London, Bernard Harty. The commitment of the Corporation to the arts in Britain – it is the third largest funder of the arts after the government and the BBC

– remains one of the unsung and unrecognised features of Britain's arts scene.

Yet these articles are not in any sense about the Barbican Centre. That subject, though fascinating in its own terms, would be too much of an arts microcosm, and in many ways an atypical one at that. They are, however, influenced by the experience of running it and learning about those problems that are common to it and to other arts institutions of many kinds. For more than three years, I have had close involvement at Board level with the Wigmore Hall, English National Opera, and the National Portrait Gallery. The insight into the way that other directors, boards and staff approach a similar raft of challenges has been extremely valuable not only in the way I have run the Barbican but in the knowledge I have gained for this book. The subjects I write about are familiar to any British arts institution, the dilemmas shared ones.

The last three years, too, have seen the reshaping of the Barbican Centre from a site whose chief characteristic was the strength and quality of its two resident institutions – the London Symphony Orchestra and the Royal Shakespeare Company – to one where the Barbican's own promotions – most notably the 'BITE '98' season in the theatre and 'Inventing America' in the concert hall – have created a third leg to our artistic stool. With the recent addition of the Barbican Art Gallery as a full part of the Centre, we are still more solidly poised to realise the potential that exists from housing 'all the arts under one roof', from having two strong resident companies as artistic partners, and from being Europe's largest arts centre.

Throughout these years of reshaping, the Barbican's Directorate team – Graham Sheffield (Arts), Ernest Newhouse (Finance), Mark Chapman (Operations), Mark Taylor (Commercial), Ruth Hasnip (Public Affairs), Diane Lennan (Personnel) and, most recently, John Hoole (Art Galleries) – have made the hard times manageable and the easier moments enjoyable. I am grateful to them for their professionalism, sense of humour and tolerance.

By a happy coincidence, the image on the cover is of the stage fittings of the Barbican Theatre. It comes from a colour transparency and light box by Catherine Yass, whose permission to use it is gratefully acknowledged. The suggestion that it would make a suitable cover was made to me by Penny Johnson, Director of the Government Art Collection who possess the work in question. My thanks to her for taking the time to give me some striking options from which to choose.

During the last three years, David Miller of Rogers Coleridge and White has been assiduous in placing several of these essays into newspapers and magazines. My thanks to him and to Deborah Rogers for actively assisting the creation of this collection.

My PA, Joanna Fyvie, deserves thanks for taking it all in her stride. Wonderfully efficient, with a memory like an elephant, she makes a reminder never seem like a nag. For ordering my time, covering my back, making the phone calls I cannot face, and generally making life possible, my fond thanks.

Finally, to state the obvious, none of this would be worth doing if the arts were not simply the most important thing in life. Everything else pales into insignificance. Standing up for them matters because Art Matters.

John Tusa, January 1999

Introduction to Paperback Edition

It was my publisher Michael Earley who warned me before publication day: 'Don't expect anyone to review the book as a whole. Everyone will seize on their particular view of art and culture and concentrate on that.' How right he was. I don't complain about the reviews – with one exception, of which more later. But I do think they missed some key points about the situation facing all the arts today.

Now, as when I first wrote, the arts are beset with the newly imposed managerial bureaucracy which wraps around all grants with a huge panoply of performance indicators in the name of accountability. The destructive effect this burden has on the essential tasks of running arts institutions properly cannot be exaggerated, has still not been questioned critically, and still needs to be part of the public debate about funding and its administration. No one wants to avoid accountability and responsibility to the paymasters and stakeholders of arts institutions, great and small. But the absence of critical questioning about the appropriateness and effectiveness of current ways of demanding that accountability is signally apparent.

What cheered me in the reaction to the book was that from fellow professionals in the arts. Many wrote to say how much the concerns I expressed closely reflected their own experiences and concerns. It was not a question of the size of the institution – some who are involved with quite small arts centres said that, slightly to their surprise, my concerns were very close to theirs. So I was not alone and know that I am not alone in worrying as I do.

And yet one reviewer, Andrew Brighton in the *Tate* magazine,

identified something about me that others did not and that I had
perhaps not fully understood about myself: 'There is something of
the awkward squad about Tusa,' he observed. I take that as a
compliment. It made me realise that years spent in journalism
devoted to scrutinising government policies and questioning
ministers and politicians had left me permanently inclined to
critical examination of everything that they say or propose. If the
application of those lifelong habits to current arts policy makes
me a member of the awkward squad, that is a position I find
pretty congenial. I have never been and could not be a
cheerleader.

Which brings me to Melvyn Bragg. (Or Mel B, Lord Spice, as
he is known.) The intemperate nature of his attack looks less
surprising a year on. Bragg's compulsive readiness in the last
twelve months to spring to the defence of New Labour's record
makes his assault on me almost predictable. It does not justify his
readiness to overlook the many areas of concern about the
funding of the arts and their public administration. It is not up to
me to suggest or search for explanations for his approach, but I do
not believe that uncritical support of government policies is the
way to improve them or to address the many fears and anxieties
that the arts world faces. If I am a member of the awkward squad,
where does Bragg stand? With the comfortable squad, I imagine.

A year on from first publication, I find the failure of critics to
home in on the possibilities of technology to expand audiences
for the arts puzzling. Some suffered a humour bypass in thinking
that I was serious about 'post-concert interviews' with orchestral
managers in the style of similar exchanges with football
managers. ('I think my first horn played a blinder tonight'; or,
'Well, a symphony is a game of four halves, if you think about it,
Gary.') Of course I do not want them to exist at the level of
screaming banality that football interviews are conducted, but
there are major questions about getting live music events onto
television which are waiting to be taken up by the arts world, arts
funders and policy makers alike, not to mention the TV
companies. In fact, the last year has seen the opportunities of
technology to transform access to the arts expand hugely. What

is now clear to me and my team at the Barbican is that every major performing space – whether concert hall or theatre – must be equipped with virtually instantly available video and audio recording and transmitting facilities.

A single set of facilities will allow a multiplicity of purposes to be served. The visual experience in the performance space itself will be enhanced; the atmosphere in the public spaces outside will be transformed; the same equipment will allow videos for marketing, promotion or education to be made; recording or live transmission onto digital side channels will come from the same source; and finally, easy audio and video access allows transmission or recording of concerts into whatever the favoured Internet music site happens to be.

Equipping major performance spaces for electronic capture of events is a major gateway project for the future of the arts. What I wrote over a year ago was on the right lines but has already been overtaken by the fresh potential of the latest technology. Collectively, the arts in Britain remain backward in seeing what the potential of this technology is, weaker still in putting it on the agenda as a matter of priority.

A year on, how do I feel the arts world stands? In an uneasy limbo. Look below the surface of almost any arts institution and you will find anxieties. Perhaps it has always been thus. But there are also – as our Marxist friends would have said – 'many contradictions, comrade'. Great new buildings; uncertain funding for keeping them working. Great artistic programming; usually done on a shoestring and a hope and a prayer. Great visions for developing the arts; limited by short-term funding provision.

And behind it all, the nagging existential doubt, far worse than any political anxiety, whether a particular government cares about the arts: does anyone care and can we expect them to if the education system and the mass media do not play their respective parts in transmitting the great inherited cultural traditions?

Now, as a year ago, those battles still need to be fought.

John Tusa, April 2000

Part One: Beliefs

1 The Arts – Can We Do Without Them?

Anniversaries, those great props of the tired editor, are also fine joggers of the memory. They remind us of time passed, of happenings overlooked, of things achieved. After fifty years, we have the opportunity to put those events into perspective. It is time to get some perspective on the arts in Britain and two major anniversaries help us to do so. Just over fifty years ago, on 12 June 1945, the Arts Council of Great Britain was created. The child of war and of the economist John Maynard Keynes, you might have thought that its half century would have found the arts in Britain bursting to celebrate the achievement of five decades of artistic patronage and development.

Some fifty years ago too, in September 1946, the Director General of the BBC, William Haley, created the Third Programme. That anniversary itself was properly and widely celebrated. It was, after all, the world's first radio network devoted to matters of art, culture and the intellect. Yet there was an angst there, as if honour was being accorded to a monument – grand of course, a tribute to its creators, a brilliant child of its time, but viewed with uncertainty by its present-day inheritors. None of the birthday tributes expressed any confidence that today's BBC would be capable of creating from scratch a Radio 3 of the existing kind or was at all equipped or inclined to do so. Still less would today's market-research-obsessed, focus-group-driven planners create anything remotely resembling the Third Programme on which Haley so confidently chanced his arm. To do so needed an unclouded, confident vision. Few of those praising the Third's birthday, myself included, bothered to conceal their fear that

Radio 3 in a recognisable form would be lucky to exist ten years from now, or that the existing funding for the BBC's orchestras – a sure bell-wether of serious cultural commitment – would survive the decade. A fine anniversary to celebrate, but was it not also the subtle ending of an era?

There was a similarly dying fall to the marking of the other great artistic anniversary, that of the Arts Council. In their annual news conference in October 1996, the then leaders of the Arts Council of England – Lord Gowrie, the Chairman, and Mary Allen, the Director General – were in no position to praise Caesar; they appeared to be preparing to bury him. There was no great celebration of fifty years of success in developing and supporting the arts. Instead Gowrie and Allen minced no words about their fears of the Treasury and its inexorable impending funding cuts – 'The Ministry of "No" ', according to Gowrie. They were openly fearful about the consequences for Britain's major performing companies if a further year of cuts in real terms was piled onto three previous years of standstill grants, leaving the recipients to make good the upward drift in inflation. A cut by any other name would cut as deep. Did the Treasury think arts organisations did not bleed? The haemorrhage in the arts was real because it represented the sapping of creative talent, the ebbing of creative energy, the wilting of creative courage. If the funding crisis of 1996 looks less acute now than it did then, that is because the Labour Government's rebasing of arts funding in the summer of 1998 has provided palliatives; it is too early to say if they are solutions. Besides, arts crises and arts funding settlements have their own cyclical pattern and this may, just may, be one of them. Far more important is the prior question of whether we need the arts at all; to answer that requires a sense of time passed, and in retreading the experience of the past, the footfall of anniversaries can help.

To start with, these calendar landmarks should jolt us by introducing some perspective. Beset as we are with a pervading sense of troubles today, we should look back at the last half-century not in anger and dismay but with wonder at an extraordinary period of arts renaissance. Fifty years ago there was no Royal Opera, no English National Opera, and no opera company in Wales, Scotland, the North of England or Ulster. Fifty years ago, there was no Royal Shakespeare Company, no Royal National Theatre, no Royal Court Theatre company. Fifty years ago, there was no Royal Festival Hall, no Barbican Centre, no Symphony Hall in Birmingham, no Orchestra Hall in Glasgow, no Bridgwater Hall in Manchester, no Grand Opera House in Belfast to name only a few.

Fifty years ago, there was no Sainsbury Wing extension to the National Gallery in London, no Museum of Modern Art in Edinburgh, no Burrell Collection in Glasgow, no Tate Gallery in either Liverpool or St Ives. The Courtauld Collection was not housed in Somerset House. Fifty years ago, the suggestion that the Tate might be contemplating a huge additional gallery space in the then still working Bankside power station would have been dismissed as arrogant and unnecessary. Fifty years ago, the prospect that the much-loved Sadler's Wells would act as cradle and midwife to the English National Opera and then be rebuilt and reborn as the nation's dedicated dance house would have been regarded as insanely visionary. The possibility that we as a nation would find ourselves in a position where we could modernise many significant arts buildings from scratch, and often build something entirely new into the bargain, would have been treated as over-heated fantasy.

Writing in 1948, T. S. Eliot was apocalyptic about the future as he viewed the post-war British cultural scene. Standards were lower than at the start of the century, he asserted: 'I see no reason why the decay of culture should not proceed much further and why we may not even anticipate a period, of some duration, of which it is possible to say that it will have no culture.' Today's cultural scene hardly bears out Eliot's gloomy predictions. It is very hard to see why he should have been so pessimistic. For, over the course of the last half-century, something has changed in the way the British regard and treat the arts – and changed hugely for the better.

Yet despite the unexpected glow induced by contemplating these outstanding five decades of achievement, the immediate problems facing the arts today are alarming. They need restating only in broad, but bleak, outline. If grants to arts institutions fail to match inflation then they are cut in real terms. The effect of that cut is not to induce economy into those institutions; it merely condemns them to ultimate financial crisis. That was the all too painful experience of the Thatcher and Major years. Recently there appears to have been some improvement in arts funding. But given the next financial crisis, the reach-me-down Treasury solution will be to put funding onto standstill again, if it is not actually cut. Another crisis will follow automatically, with theatres, orchestras, dance and opera companies cutting costs and activity savagely in order to balance their books. That is one lesson repeatedly taught over the last fifty years.

For cuts in grants always lead to cuts in performances, reductions in quality, weakened activity, more cautious planning, less imagination and risk-taking; less time is devoted to the arts activity, more time spent on fund-raising, budget-balancing, sponsorship-raising and sacking. As a policy, it is not even respectable in economic terms. Pretending that any institution can find what are called 'efficiency gains' on a continual basis year after year is the economics of the peasant's milch-cow. The thrifty peasant boasted to his neighbours that each year he saved money by feeding his cow a bit less fodder. It worked triumphantly well until one day – to the peasant's evident amazement – the cow dropped dead. That is the situation to which most arts institutions are subjected. Do not be surprised when they start to keel over. Remember, too, that during the years when the cow was fed less and less, its constant moos of complaint were disparaged as mere 'whingeing'.

Do not believe anyone who says that the arts are spendthrift. They do not have that option. Most top-class British actors and actresses are paid a weekly wage rather less than the daily charge-out rate of the management consultants constantly inflicted upon them. Most singers – good ones at that – are not paid as Pavarotti or Domingo or Jessye Norman or Angela Gheorghiu are paid. Though, incidentally, if you work in a profession where you are asked to fly from California in order to sing the Count in *Figaro* at a couple of hours' notice, go to the theatre sleepless and jetlagged, and find that you have never even seen your Countess before, then that is surely worth a bob or two.

Most orchestral players are wretchedly paid and get many noughts removed from the fees demanded by the top-rank soloists. For four years, between 1995 and 1999, the rank-and-file players in Britain's best orchestra, the London Symphony Orchestra, accepted a wages standstill because the Arts Council grant was frozen. Nor are audiences, decried as 'middle-class' by some, particularly well-heeled. Most of those who attend plays, concerts, dance, opera or galleries are not paying the super-gala prices for their seats, but sums lower than those for a West End musical or rock show, and well below the cost of a seat at a Premier League football match. Half the seats at the Coliseum, the home of English National Opera, cost less than £25; a seat at West Ham for a Premier League football match is £27. I will not hear a word said against the team I have supported since a boy, but the £25 spent on opera at the Coliseum usually yields more drama and entertainment, not to mention better singing, than at Upton Park. Before the Royal Opera closed, more people went there in a year than went to watch West Ham at home. (The players at Upton Park are almost as international.) What those figures clearly demonstrate is that the idea of the arts as a ghetto of financial or any other kind of privilege simply bears no relationship to who makes up the audiences and what their pleasure costs them.

When the Lottery grant of some £30 million for the redevelopment of Sadler's Wells was announced in October 1995, the press reaction was, sadly, predictable. Photographers were despatched to the evening performance to witness dinner-jacketed nobs landing from their limos, or taking the interval air with their champagne. To their picture editors' chagrin what they found was a dance audience of the young and the black, casually dressed, coolly drinking beer from the bottle – a far cry from the hoped-for image of privileged and subsidised luxury. Few shutters clicked; no pictures appeared thereafter. It was the wrong story. The reality, which the newspapers would not face, is of a vastly diverse, cheerfully informal, seriously inclined, well informed body of people, carefully allocating to the arts the comparatively small sum of money they have available for discretionary spending. Fifty years of increasing the provision of the highest quality arts has created that audience. Oddly, it has not created an equivalent popular acceptance of that fact. The audience, as Lord Gowrie once observed, is not an elite – the arts are not for elites; but they are conducted by elites, by the best, just as any other human activity, sport not least, is conducted by the best.

And, despite insinuations to the contrary, the arts do not make unreasonable demands on the national purse. Some forty years ago, in 1956, an Arts Council pamphlet celebrating its first decade noted that direct funding through the Council was a tiny fraction of the sums directly spent on education, libraries, galleries and museums. If only, it suggested, half of one per cent of that figure were given to the Council, then the resulting princely uninflated total sum of £2½ million a year would transform the whole position of arts funding. Forty years on, Lord Gowrie ventured a similar proposal. The arts, he suggested in January 1995 at the Royal Society of Arts, should receive one per cent of present total public spending, to be indexed at two per cent a year. That would yield a massive extra £700 million annually. A modest proposal or a mite ambitious; it was undoubtedly visionary. Yet the proposition that even such a sizeable additional grant to the arts might unbalance government expenditure or control of the public finances is too ludicrous to take seriously.

Of course the arts institutions have always wanted more and need more. They want more in order to meet the needs of audiences more effectively. Over fifty years, if any politician took the long view, the arts have used increased expenditure imaginatively, creatively and effectively. At the present juncture, however, though the arts certainly need more money to do their job better, what they most want is what British industry begged successive governments for: stability and predictability so that they can plan ahead and do their job properly. The Blair

Government and the Chancellor of the Exchequer, Gordon Brown, now appear to understand some of industry's argument for these conditions. But the suspicion remains that the need for financial stability for the arts has not yet been fully taken on board. The powers that be do not seem to know that orchestras and opera companies have to plan four or five years ahead, at least as far in advance as major industries. To do so efficiently, they have to know roughly how much money they will have to spend.

However, the true heart of the uneasy national debate about arts funding is not about money as such nor the way it is allocated. The basic problem lies in the public approach towards the arts as a whole. We are faced less with a question of 'how much' to give, than 'whether to give' at all. The shortage of money reflects a fundamental unease about arts provision in its essence. Fifty years on, the case, it seems, has to be made once again, and constantly. 'Why the Arts?' Do we need them? Why do we have to pay for them? Fifty years on, Britain's internal debate about the place of arts in society is as intense, confused and unresolved as it ever was. In his first policy speech, the new Chairman of the Arts Council of England, Gerry Robinson, called for a debate about the arts. It will surely take place but not necessarily on terms that he will like and certainly not on the narrow terms that he so arbitrarily defined.*

As a start to that debate, it is worthwhile returning to the early years. The great and once again fashionable economist, John Maynard Keynes, the first Chairman of the Arts Council, was severely realistic about arts funding. As he offered to pay from his own pocket the first two-thirds of the cost of the new Arts Theatre in Cambridge in 1935, he observed to his wife, Lydia Lopokova: 'The greatest comfort of all, I think, from having money . . . is that one does not need to badger other people for it.' Not for Keynes the need to pester the rich or well-disposed to make good the shortcomings of public provision for the arts. No one now calculates the opportunity cost to British intellectual

---

* See Chapter Ten.

life if Keynes had had to spend more time fund-raising and less
time thinking, lecturing and writing.

For Keynes, it was an article of belief that a university needed
a theatre in exactly the same way as the sciences needed
laboratories. Only in a theatre could the complicated depend-
ence of drama upon literature, music and design be put to the test
and understood. As to the arts as a whole, he saw their
justification in philosophical beliefs which held that goodness in
society increased as a result of the amount of beauty. While there
are many who still subscribe to such beliefs, only the very naive
would think that they cut any ice with a Treasury devoted to
strict financial prudence, still less that large claims about the
absolute value of beauty can be presented without challenge or
dispute. An assertion of this kind today would walk straight into
the reductive comment: 'Well, since there is so much more of
what you call art around, why is there still so much crime today?'
Still, those grander and more absolute propositions were good
enough in their time and persuasive enough to establish a process
of arts funding that still survives – however uncertainly. By
contrast, in today's more sceptical, less idealistic world, the more
the arts articulate their 'Vision', the less public imagination there
is devoted to funding and turning that vision into reality.

Fifty years ago, as Keynes's Arts Council started work, the
founders of the BBC Third Programme were wrestling with
similar questions about the national need for culture. Vision they
had; commitment they would deliver; but doubts they acknowledged. In fact, the continuing internal and external debate about
culture and the arts within the BBC mirrored national doubts in
precise form. In 1946, the BBC decided to pay a price for culture
– too high a price some said even at the time – and insisted that
it was a price worth paying. William Haley, the then Director
General, said that he saw every civilised nation as a cultural
pyramid with 'a lamentable broad base and a lamentable narrow
tip'. Yet the pyramid was not a static one, but culturally upwardly
mobile. 'My conception was of a BBC through the years – many
years – which would slowly move listeners from one stratum of
this pyramid to the next.'

If the wish to be open and inclusive is one that we would recognise today, Haley's terms of reference for the new pro-gramme (what we would call the Mission Statement in today's jargon) were more austere and unyielding and, in contrast to other comments, appeared to accept the inevitable exclusion of some in his definition of the target listeners: 'The programme is designed to be of artistic and cultural importance. The audience envisaged is one already aware of artistic experience and will include persons of taste, of intelligence, and of education; it is, therefore, selective and not casual, and both attentive and critical.'

Such were the foundations on which a cornucopia of music, talk and drama was unloaded onto a nation which had never enjoyed anything like it before. Haley had no illusions about the likely popularity of the programme. But he and his supporters were supremely self-confident in their values and their concept of culture. No one fifty years ago had to qualify the word by explaining why culture did not mean 'pop' culture, or 'mass' culture or 'lifestyle' culture or 'club' culture. For Haley and the intellectual middle class, it meant the great continuum of inherited Western creative artistic activity of which they were an instinctive part; it required no further definition, as it does today. It certainly required no apology, as it would now. All the terms of the debate were simpler fifty years ago. In a public speech, Haley noted with disdain that 'the surest way to increase the number of listeners is to debase the standards', a statement with powerful echoes today of the debate about 'dumbing down' by constantly lowering expectations of 'what the audience will take'. Reflecting on Haley's comment, the *Newcastle Journal* observed at the time: 'We are, in general, a low-brow rather than a high-brow people. We should aim, at least, at being soundly middle-brow people, with aspirations towards higher planes.' How different social rhetoric is today: at a time when the middle classes, in financial terms, have never been larger, and the manual working classes are almost a thing of the past, few in public life would care to claim anything but some working-class origins and considerable satisfaction with mass tastes.

Haley's view of culture, indeed the general view of culture half a century ago, was far narrower than it is today. We have absorbed some aspects of pop culture into painting, music, literature and dance. While there is proper debate about the way that pop integrates itself, we are more broad-minded in our readiness to extend the frontiers that define art. There is, too, a greater readiness to include influences from around the world into the activities that could once be simply defined as Western culture. Such eclecticism was a long way from the intellectual world of the post-war era.

It remains remarkable that the BBC should create a project like the Third Programme on such confident, almost insouciant foundations. But if there is an overriding explanation for the comparative ease with which Haley could state and win the case for setting up the Third Programme, it is to be found in the unifying experience of the war and the nation's intensified cultural experience during those years.

In 1939, when CEMA, the Committee for the Encouragement of Music and the Arts was created, it was an emergency operation to save the arts from total black-out – literal and metaphorical. Many of its aims were very practical: to keep up public morale; to entertain bored evacuees, shift workers and servicemen waiting for action; to keep artistes in employment; and, almost as an afterthought, to spread knowledge of and enjoyment of the arts themselves. Under the CEMA umbrella, the Old Vic had three touring companies on the road playing one-night stands in town halls, miners' institutes, and factory hostels. In 1940, a travelling exhibition called 'Art for the People' attracted 300,000 visitors during its journey through 80 villages and country towns. By 1944, CEMA provided no fewer than 6,140 concerts of which 840 were symphony concerts. Granted that many of the audiences had nothing else to do, and conceding that not all experienced a sudden conversion to the fine arts, this somewhat forced wartime exposure to them had a revolutionary and lasting effect in building a new national cultural base. From today's perspective, the CEMA initiative has a very *dirigiste* feel to it, paternalist, prescriptive. Yet just as food rationing delivered striking improvements in public health, and utility clothing put decent clothes on the backs of rich and poor alike, CEMA presented good quality to all – and, in so doing, not only broadened public appreciation of the arts but increased people's desire to experience more. A foundation was built.

So successful was CEMA in creating a new audience, that the Arts Council evolved speedily from it as the war ended. Keynes believed that the new council would 'carry the arts throughout the countryside and maintain metropolitan standards' – both ideals that have informed arts policy ever since. Though many today would see his remark as patronising to the regions, for Keynes it only meant sharing access to the best available. Despite his belief in the widespread availability of the arts, Keynes was not, according to Kenneth Clark, 'a man for wandering minstrels and amateur theatricals. He believed in excellence.' Many believed that after the hideous dangers and sufferings of the war, the nation deserved something better. That included the arts. The wartime possibility of death or captivity sharpened the appetite for life and art hugely.

It was against this broader national background of an appetite awakened that the Third Programme was born. Despite constant niggles at the smallness of the audience, and its disproportionate cost – disproportionate, that is, to the rest of radio – the BBC persevered over the decades with a third network of some kind or another, tacking and trimming to the prevailing financial and artistic winds but trying to keep intact a recognisably cultural network with terms of reference beyond those of its more mainstream or populist partners. There were repeated attempts to define why the arts were worth undertaking and continuing. For a while, those definitions changed little.

When a former BBC Controller of Music, Robert Ponsonby, wrote that 'what is unarguable is that the BBC should be unreservedly committed to a radio channel devoted to music and the arts at a discriminating level of quality, intelligence and articulacy', his vocabulary and approach were not that different from Haley's forty years earlier. When, however, the former Controller of BBC Radio 3, Nicholas Kenyon observed in 1998 that 'the tension between highbrow culture and popular culture and the cost of what we do and the number of people who use it' has changed little over fifty years, he exposed the distance still to go before the arts have an assured place in Britain. The future and the nature of Radio 3 will remain the white flag in the nation's cultural tug of war. It is a battle still to be fought, a battle still to be won.

The evidence of the BBC's fifty-year-long internal and public debate about Radio 3 demonstrates that abstract claims for the arts cast in absolute terms have not got them or their argument very far. The unconvinced remain unconvinced. In this respect, the pragmatic, utilitarian British – or is it the English? – are utterly different from their continental cousins. It is as if the British are guilty about supporting the arts, or worse still, simply agnostic. As a result, in the last decade and a half, the arts have jumped through a series of hoops trying to convince the public that they are worth paying for. The process has been often educative, occasionally undignified and ultimately ineffective. The implied case for the last half century that the arts were good in themselves has been rudely set aside as other, and perhaps unsuitable, criteria have been introduced. The fact that they have been imposed at all suggests a general failure by all of us in the arts to justify our *raison d'être* in terms that command political and public support.

The difficulties began in 1983 when the recently created National Audit Office introduced fresh ways of looking at the finances of the arts. Using the still novel criteria of 'economy, efficiency and effectiveness' which it applies without fear or favour to all the institutions it scrutinises, the NAO made Performance Indicators the yardsticks of effectiveness, Forward Plans with Specific Activity Targets the measures of efficiency, and tougher accounting systems the guarantors of economy. We were in a new world. We were no longer the arts, pure and simple, but rather part of a great national cultural industry, just another sector of the economy. The Whitehall managerial revolution did not single out the arts for special attention; its working methods applied to all and sundry.

In 1985, the Arts Council Chairman, William Rees-Mogg, took the hint. Deploying the new managerialism with relish, in his lecture entitled 'The Political Economy of the Arts', Rees-Mogg stated: 'The Arts Council gives the best value for money in job creation of any part of the state system . . . The arts are to Britain what the sun is to Spain.' It was a good try but failed to notice two facts: first, the Thatcher Government was less interested in job creation (the traditional cry of the unions) and only in wealth creation; and, second, everybody in Spain liked and enjoyed the sun which comes free in any case.

In 1985, the Arts Council tried again, proclaiming the arts to be 'The Great British Success Story', and issuing 'an invitation to the nation to invest in the arts'. Unlike all other privatisation issues, that prospectus was distinctly undersubscribed. Nobody felt inclined to 'Tell Sid' to put his money in there in a hurry. In 1986, the Council tried still harder. 'Partnership: Making Arts Money Work Harder.' The language used to argue the arts case changed. We no longer promoted concerts, mounted exhibitions or put on a production of a play; we delivered 'product'. Gone were the days when visitors went to galleries, audiences attended concerts or the theatre; they were all 'customers'. An arts institution – if it knew what was good for it – 'delivered product to the customer'. Subsidy or public patronage were out-of-date words; the arts were looking for 'investment'. In these new cant terms, a well-managed arts institution would deliver 'a properly focused and researched product, appropriately diverse for its particular clients, consistent with its vision and targets while working to externally agreed and objectively measurable perform-ance indicators'. By 1998, the Arts Council Chairman, Gerry Robinson, was impatiently demanding an end to 'an assembly of wish lists from every part of the arts constituency'. He insisted on a 'limited amount of deliverable priorities'.

The trouble is that – then and now – the language is all wrong. It is not merely that it is not ours; it is not appropriate to our activity. A member of an audience expects good service but is buying an experience – a very different thing. A product is a predictable, quantifiable object which is expected to perform jobs, tasks or functions. A play, dance, opera, exhibition or concert offers something varied, variable, untried or tested, often unpredictable and occasionally experimental. But the real trap in the dialogue of the 1980s occurred with the word 'investment'. As the arts world queued up with its list of proposed investments, there was one response: 'What is the return on the investment?' To which the only answer was: 'There is no return on the investment in the sense that the word is properly understood.' Back came the reply: 'Then why are you asking us to invest in you at all?' Words matter. Vocabulary must be appropriate and we will get nowhere by using words which conceal what we are and why we do what we do.

Using managerial vocabulary has never yet produced great art. History suggests the reverse. Supposing Diaghilev had had to work within the parameters of such vocabulary, would he have created *Firebird*, *Petrouchka* or *The Rite of Spring*? What would the twentieth century have been without the music that Diaghilev commissioned from Stravinsky, or the designers like Bakst or choreographers like Massine and Fokine who mounted the ballets? Theirs was the dialogue of art – while Diaghilev was always a canny businessman. If the basic language is that of business, can the result be art? Occasionally, perhaps, but only if you mind your concepts, and realise that business theories are instruments rather than ends. Too often in recent years, the arts have behaved as if they will only be taken seriously if they lean over backwards and pretend to be what they are not. We may have some of an industry's characteristics, but we remain essentially different. Unless that difference is stated and restated, then the wind will change and we will end up thinking of ourselves as a business, behaving like one too and forgetting our responsibilities to art.

Let us do a deal. We in the arts will not resist the business jargon that has been forced upon us. It is not difficult to use; all too easy in fact. Many of its principles do help you to run the theatre, the orchestra or the gallery in a business-like manner. But we will only talk like a business if our interlocutors accept that we are different. We will learn their tricks and not shy away from some of their vocabulary; but they in return must understand what distinguishes and separates us.

The arts continue to wriggle with a series of instrumental arguments – all turning on the proposition that they should be supported not because of what they are but because of the impact they have. In 1986, the Arts Council's 'Partnership' document held up the arts as an instrument of urban renewal. Inner cities would be revived, cultural industries would grow as a result, and employment would follow. True enough. Education would improve too. As arts and musical education faltered in schools, arts institutions must carry out emergency, remedial work. Without an education programme, would there be an audience in a decade's time? This case for the arts turns them into a kind of super-welfare industry, another arm of Treasury economic regeneration policy, a part of the enterprise culture. If they are to be all these things, is there any room or time for being what they should be: institutions and people striving for the highest possible artistic achievement?

By 1988, the economic argument was in full flood. A Policy Studies Institute paper called 'The Economic Importance of the Arts in Britain' recorded a gross turnover from the arts sector of £10 billion; it employed 500,000 people directly; accounted for 1.28% of gross domestic product; and ranked fourth in the list of invisible export-earners. Think, too, how much the state earned in VAT and taxes, in taking people out of costly unemployment. Later still, the arts were presented as a key component in the transition from an industrial to a post-industrial society, in the evolution from a working society to a leisure society, and in the generation of economic multiplier effects – if a successful theatre opens, the nearby leisure and dining quarter follows.

These arguments – barring a few quibbles about what was included in the figures – were neither inaccurate nor invalid. At the time they seemed novel, impressive and weighty. Even so, they were inadequate for raising arts funding onto a new level, where stability and predictability could be relied upon. Worst of all, the arts had fallen into the trap of arguing on the other side's ground and terms. They were bound to lose. They still begged the question, 'Why the arts at all?' Of course, they were useful 'as parts of the economy' but other great industries that had once justified themselves by creating a lot of jobs had been closed; why should the arts be special? Over the last fifty years, the arts scene has been transformed and for the better; yet one thing has not changed: the fundamental questioning of the arts and the demand that if they claim to be special, they must make the claim for special treatment stick. Everyone involved in the arts must make their own attempt at such a justification.

Here is my own attempt.

The arts matter because they are universal; because they are non-material; because they deal with daily experience in a transforming way; because they question the way we look at the world; because they offer different explanations of that world; because they link us to our past and open the door to the future; because they work beyond and outside routine categories; because they take us out of ourselves; because they make order out of disorder and stir up the stagnant; because they offer a shared experience rather than an isolated one; because they encourage the imagination, and attempt the pointless; because they offer beauty and confront us with the fact of ugliness; because they suggest explanations but no solutions; because they present a vision of integration rather than disintegration; because they force us to think about the difference between the good and the bad, the false and the true. The arts matter because they embrace, express and define the soul of a civilisation. A nation without arts would be a nation that had stopped talking to itself, stopped dreaming, and had lost interest in the past and lacked curiosity about the future.

The question of why the arts matter cannot be answered on the back of a Kellogg's Cornflakes packet – or if it can, then I have certainly not won the competition. Matthew Arnold defined the arts as 'the best that has been thought and said in the world', and of course the best sung, acted, danced, painted and performed in any way. William Blake, quoted by Robert Hewison in his excellent book *Culture and Consensus*, stated: 'Let it be no more said that the States encourage Arts; for it is the Arts that encourage States.' Let the present-day British state allow itself a moment of encouragement by permitting the arts to flourish. It does not involve a huge financial risk; the experience of the last fifty years demonstrates the effectiveness with which the arts have created an entirely new landscape in Britain for creativity. Rather, any risk involved to the British economy or the well-being of the state lies entirely in under-providing for the arts today and having to pick up the pieces tomorrow.

Not long ago, I was discussing such ideas with a dinner companion whom I had never met before. Was she worried about the arts today? She said that her recurring nightmare, one that she had dreamed throughout her life, was of a darkness into which broken fragments of pictures and musical instruments were hurtling. Through it she felt a personal sense of disintegration. I believe that a society where pictures and music – and everything else in the great body of the arts – have gone to pieces through neglect or indifference would be darkness indeed.

More recently, I asked a distinguished British composer what would happen if there was a moratorium on the playing or performance of music composed before 1920. Would we not, I suggested, return to it after the moratorium with a renewed sense of its value and the essential part it plays in our lives? No, he replied bleakly; we would never return to it at all.

Are things so perilously balanced between continuity and extinction? I do not believe so. But we have both to defend the arts and, better still, explain them in ways that do justice to them for what they are rather than diminish them. T. S. Eliot was wrong fifty years ago when he was struck by the utter barrenness of the cultural outlook in Britain. We should not assume that without passionate and determined advocacy he might not be right in the next fifty years.

2 The Arts in the Twenty-First Century – The Agony or the Ecstasy?

I have a dream, or is it a nightmare? Of a world without arts – and therefore without arts centres. It will come true in the next century, probably within a few years of its starting. Do not worry then about how to run arts centres, how to programme them, market them, or publicise them. Do not fret about audiences – they will be 'customers'; do not anguish about promoting plays, dance or concerts – they will be merely 'product'; do not agonise about audience response – concentrate on 'customer satisfaction'; do not worry about how well you are doing – just ask whether you are meeting your 'performance indicators', 'measuring outcome against promised deliverables'. If you devise an arts season, you will first have to show that you have a 'viable exit strategy'. As you plan your programmes, never forget to ask yourself if you are adequately 'penetrating the core repertoire'. If the audience liked something once, all you will have to do is give it to them again. Undermined by such vocabulary, sapped by such assumptions, in the twenty-first century art will be obsolete. So will arts centres.

There are various pressing reasons for taking such a pessimistic view. None of them are fanciful. All of them relate to theories, practices and principles that exist today and will gain ground and strength over the years. As the arts wilt under the relentless pressure from the experience of the mass electronic media, so the charge of elitism – in the sense of social and financial exclusiveness – will grow. The more elitist the arts are accused of being – no matter how unfairly – the more difficult it will be to justify spending government money – the taxpayers' money, after all – on them. Market testing and consumer research will erode and undermine artistic judgement as it is enfeebling editorial vision in the BBC. Targets will be set for attendances at arts events. Research will establish what sort of programmes will hit the bull's-eye. Events that clearly miss will be excluded because they stop the business plan being fulfilled. Independent artistic activity will be undermined. So will the taking of risk.

Other current trends point further to such pessimistic conclusions. The funding of arts activities will be determined by quotas – regional quotas, educational quotas, ethnic quotas, disabled quotas, interest group quotas. Anyone who claims to be excluded from the range of activities mounted by an arts centre will be listened to more than those who are satisfied with them. Conversely – but at the same time – unless the provision of arts and the satisfaction derived from them are demonstrated as being universal, they will be deemed to be discriminatory and inadequate.

Above all, the arts – like education – will have to be judged 'relevant'. Unless their utility and immediate comprehensibility to the broad public is demonstrated, then the time, space and money spent on them will be questioned or eliminated. Just as dangerous: arts organisations will have to demonstrate the value of the 'opportunity cost' of the various assets devoted to them. Since those investments can invariably get quicker, surer, more obvious returns from other activities, the arts will sink under the weight of their perceived failure to optimise the use of scarce resources.

So the arts and arts centres, previously cut loose from their intellectual moorings by current ways of thinking, will ebb away in a tide of indifference compounded with actual hostility. They already stand naked and without defence in a world where what cannot be measured is not valued; where what cannot be predicted will not be risked; where what cannot be controlled will not be permitted; where what cannot deliver a forecast outcome is not undertaken; where what does not belong to all will be allowed to none. That is the agony.

For we have lost a vocabulary and an area of permitted public discourse where values are valued rather than costed; where

inspiration is regarded as heaven-sent rather than an unacceptable risk. Instead, we have a materialistic debate where the
immaterial is dismissed as pretentious rather than welcomed as
essential; where art for art's sake is pigeon-holed as a personal
obsession rather than recognised as a vital social ingredient;
where the public good is dismissed as a chimera so long as it
cannot be quantified on a balance sheet.

But when my nightmare/dream comes true, there will of course
still be ecstasy, or whatever its latest chemical form happens to
be. Plenty of that. Immediate, constant, diversionary, entertaining, in ever growing intensity in ever growing forms, on an ever
growing number of occasions.

Of course, these are all deliberate, provocative exaggerations,
aren't they? Not altogether. I am also deadly serious, and so
should we all be, about the dangers that exist in the public
debate where we have to defend, promote and justify the
activities of the arts. It is not that anyone involved wants to buck
the currently predominant managerial culture – we do not. It is
not difficult to learn. Everyone in the arts above all has a pressing
need and obligation to use the little money they have as well as
they can. But managerialism should be a tool rather than an end;
a method rather than an absolute; a rule of thumb rather than a
tablet of stone; a system of analysis rather than a panacea for
every problem. If applied without discrimination, managerial
vocabulary and methods threaten to swamp the work that they
are, overtly, intended to support. They become the master not
the servant. They are a necessary part of our lives but are far from
sufficient in themselves to make a good arts centre or to allow
great art to be created.

Even once that assumption is accepted, once the high priests
of managerialism and their highly-priced acolytes, the consultants, are put in their rightful place, the questions anyone
involved in running an arts centre must answer in the next
century are legion. They can be presented as a set of antithetical
challenges that must be addressed and if possible resolved: the
claims of Continuity versus the attractions of Novelty; the
demands of Memory versus the attractions of Sensation; the calm

of Apollo versus the frenzy of Dionysus; the nagging of Curiosity versus the lure of Reassurance; the necessity of Diversity versus the ease of Homogenisation. Where will we define the role and purpose of arts centres in relation to these philosophical co-ordinates?

Continuity versus Novelty. I choose the word 'novelty' deliberately and carefully. I do not mean 'innovation', which I define as the continuous building on, and evolution of, a past continuum of creative work and activity. Novelty is something very different; the pursuit of the merely new, the strange, the curious, with little or no reference to and sometimes a total rejection of the past. This kind of novelty is pursued for its own sake rather than as a new way of listening, of opening minds, or intensifying experience. Arts centres will have the choice or necessity of deciding the balance between continuity and innovation on one side and sheer novelty on the other. They will be coerced into pursuing novelty precisely because it is unencumbered by the past and because its pursuit and presentation can be engaged in without the bore of referring to or learning about the past.

No tradition of the arts – at least in the Western world – has been able to survive without taking forward what has been achieved and developing it in new and untried directions, in short without innovation. To date, most arts organisations have kept a balance between the performance and the maintenance of the great canon of Western art-works and the process of extending that tradition. A sense of history and the historical achievement is not incompatible with innovation, rather it plays an essential part in it. I asked the celebrated German composer, Hans Werner Henze, an arch-modernist to many, where he saw his musical roots. He replied unhesitatingly: 'My roots are with Beethoven!' What is under increasing threat is devotion to, respect for, and teaching of the centuries of artistic achievement which underpin all art forms. The past is regarded by too many people as just that – gone, and so different from modern sensibilities, experience and outlook as to be irrelevant to behaviour and understanding. The wholly new on the other hand is immediate, sensational, value-free, unencumbered by comparison, and skilfully tailored to contemporary sensibilities. It rejects the validity of any critical comparison as being too deferential to a rejected past. The wholly new deflects any suggestion of value judgement with the disarming defence that whatever is done is intended ironically, knowingly and therefore incorporates its own judgements within itself.

As the education process seems to place an ever greater emphasis on personal expression rather than systematic learning, absorbing knowledge of the historical artistic canon seems more and more burdensome, less a pillar of support, and more a dead-weight of needless obligation. The audience for the artistic presentation of the historical canon and those activities that grow from it will wither because less has been taught and therefore less is understood. Arts centres have to choose where they stand in this process and defend their decisions.

That means they will also have to reconcile the conflicting demands of Memory and Sensation. Will arts centres carry in themselves a sense of the past rather than a mere indulgence in the present, deliberately retaining awareness of tradition rather than a monochrome existence in the everyday? Arts centres are not just places where a nod to the past is an intrinsic and essential part of the work of the present, but where a knowledge of what has been done in the past is an essential and precious building brick in the creation of art today. At the very least, knowing where to pick and choose in the immeasurably rich traditions of the past should be part of the atmosphere sustained and presented by an arts centre. Those who think they can dispense with any knowledge of the artistic past are as shallow as they are presumptuous. Will arts centres hold to such a position in the face of those who insist that today we know everything, that it is easily stored on a computer, is readily available to everybody and that this obviates the need for any sustained or organised engagement with or understanding of the past?

While they decide, they will have to bear in mind a tension that exists between two other demands – those of Curiosity and Reassurance. Arts centres know that much of the best that they must offer in order to justify survival will challenge, understanding, develop experience, and be driven by innovation and curiosity. But will they offer it? For this is a difficult pitch to make. It assumes a willingness on the part of audiences to reach beyond the familiar in form and subject matter. Elsewhere, much of contemporary mass culture is driven by an overwhelming wish to provide the blandly reassuring. Elsewhere, too, much that is trivial is excused or justified on the grounds that everyone knows that 'it is all a giggle' or ironic.

And while all the conflicts are being mediated, all the opposing claims met, another feud tears the arts centres. Never mind the false gods, with which true god will they stand? With calm Apollo or with frenzied Dionysus? In 1968, the musical *Hair* declared the dawning of a new age – the age of Aquarius, of feelings and instinct, of non-rationality and freedom from restraint or inhibition. Today, we can express that trend differently through classical mythology rather than astrology. For society has rediscovered the appeal of Dionysus. Extreme self-expression, encouraged into ecstatic states by ever new classes of designer drugs, is an increasingly accepted – or at least unchallenged – form of leisure activity. The escape from reason does not have to be chemical. Group hysteria, cultural alcoholia, new instant 'religions' such as 'Dianism' are just as attractive, distracting and 'alternative'. Whatever the nature of the original stimulus, mind and thought are deliberately abandoned in a regular, systematic indulgence in non-cerebral activities. An alleged natural urge for togetherness is pursued and delivered in an atmosphere of often synthetically induced, physical ecstasy. The fallible, imperfect, inadequate but precious human interactions that make up true community are rejected and substituted by a beguiling chemical buzz of illusion, noise, electronic sensory deprivation and ultimately by delusion.

The Apollonian qualities – rational, pensive, cool, inquiring, reserved, dispassionate – are in much more limited demand. Acknowledging the fact that all art involves a constant interplay between the two spirits, it has to be accepted that by comparison with the unbridled Dionysiac atmosphere of much of today's leisure and entertainment world, the arts, even at their most uninhibited, fall squarely into Apollo's camp. Here there is an underlying belief in qualities other than instant, constant and unreflecting self-gratification. Where will arts centres ultimately place themselves between these two competing gods? Will they decide that unless they offer some of the atmosphere of clubbing, they will be bypassed and rejected? If they do not, they must bear in mind the fate of the opponents of Bacchus in the *Bacchae* who were ultimately torn apart in a frenzy by the Maenads. Those who totally ignore Bacchus/Dionysus do so at their peril.

So if my dream or nightmare does come true, will purpose-built premises for the arts be value-free zones because the determination of worth has been abandoned on the grounds that attempting to separate the good from the bad is too difficult, unfashionably prescriptive or even allegedly intellectually oppressive? In a society where values are relative, why should anyone bother with matters such as the good and the bad? Or will they keep up a commitment to a flow of value-led activity strongly rooted in the past even as it risks disturbing its audiences?

How, too, will we meet the demands of Diversity versus Homogenisation? Are we to rest content with a world made safe for Macfood and Waltculture and Rupertnews and Tedvision? Will we lie down meekly before the warriors of globalisation who impose a new totalitarianism of taste, thought, experience and views decking out self-serving economic arguments in the pseudo-democratic clothing of freedom and choice? Or will arts centres speak out for and make possible the practice, the expression of the local, the particular, the individual, the differentiated, while rejecting the formulaic that is the trademark of the global endeavour? True art is universal but not homogenised – its diversity being one element in its richness. Global culture snuffs out categories of artistic endeavour as surely as global enterprise threatens the bio-diversity of natural species.

Such are the questions that really underlie all of our activities and challenge all our assumptions in the future. How we solve them will vary from individual to individual and flow from decisions as to what the arts are about. Why do we bother with them? Why do millions of viewers, listeners, audience members engage in them at all? We all have our private answers and we should make them rather more public. We must reclaim the area of public discourse on the arts from the managers and consultants. How would I do it? Something like this.

Art is about searching and sometimes finding; it defines pain and sorrow and sometimes softens them; it is about exploring confusion and defining disorder; it is about sharing the private and listening to silence; it is lasting but not immediate; it is valuable but priceless; it is based in the past but reaches for the future; it is free to anybody but may not be used by everybody; it is universal though it may be attacked as exclusive; it is diverse and not homogenised; it resists categories and makes connections across them. Art is all the things that the rest of life is not.

I cannot conceive of a century, a decade, a year, a minute of the future without it. Surely, neither can anyone else if they think about it seriously. But the dream will end as a nightmare unless we take it seriously.

3 When I Hear the Word Culture, I Reach for My Identity

Put together two British arts directors today and they talk of money. The British arts scene is overwhelmed by issues of funding, with the micro questions of subsidy and the macro questions of survival. These problems are obsessive, corroding, destructive and inward-looking. The prospect of hanging may concentrate a man's mind wonderfully, but the prospect of cultural extinction concentrates the mind on nothing useful. Above all, the induced parochialism is particularly sad. The importance of arts and culture in the political scene, and their valuable contribution to the European dimension, are easy to overlook. As an integral part of the culture and history of Europe, we are constantly linked with our European colleagues in a vast nexus of arts exchanges, activities and projects. Yet we seldom reflect on these connections and their value both in the narrow cultural sense and in the contribution they make to the wider European debate.

Defining European cultural identity is a challenge of its own. Even without too specific a definition, thinking about the contribution that existing cultural experience makes to the political task of forging a new Europe is worthwhile, if only because it forces us to raise our horizons beyond our own seemingly ever-present miseries. (By the by, I use the word 'forging' with reluctance and not only because it is a part of official Eurospeak. Its overtones of Stalinist-Leninist brute force in the shaping of events and institutions is too uncomfortable for my own evolutionary taste.)

These thoughts were sharpened by listening to Eurocrats and Euro-enthusiasts at a conference in Prague in March 1998, organised by the British Council. From Lithuania in the Baltic to Slovenia in the Adriatic, the new democracies of the former socialist bloc are desperate to become members of the European Union. For Eurocrats, though, keenness to join the Club is not enough. Without commitment to the ideal, membership would be as shallowly rooted as that of Irish 'stockpot Protestants' who changed their religion in famine-struck Ireland in the nineteenth century not because of a sudden conversion of faith but because it was better than starving. As Eurocrats wrestle with the task of creating true adherence to the European Union in the countries of Central and Eastern Europe, the notion that a millennium or so of European cultural activity might be a good way of reinforcing and popularising the process of widening and deepening Europe has not featured strongly in what has been an overwhelmingly politicised process.

For Eurocrats, the bedrock idea of 'being European' centres upon dedication to the rule of law, human rights and democracy. There is no difficulty about this 'motherhood and apple pie' concept, except that many countries in the former socialist camp still do not enjoy motherhood or apple pie in nourishing quantities. Beyond this, joining and identifying with the new European institutions – the European Parliament, Court of Human Rights, and European Commission – are regarded as almost as important in creating that broader European consciousness. But the thought that Europe's sheer cultural homogeneity might be used to build European identity struck this collection of Eurocrats gathered in Prague with considerable surprise. Does Europe, in the Brussels sense, have an underused instrument for creating union: Europe's common culture? I think it does.

There is a second, more challenging question. If culture is called into play in the political arena, could the livelier sense of a European identity help to set into perspective some of its destructive ethnic rivalries? A sense of a European culture might achieve two apparently contradictory aims; to protect local cultures from being swallowed up in the global mass and to prevent those local cultures themselves from turning inward, rancid and excessively particular, by placing them firmly in a larger European context. That larger framework would serve to reassure rather than to overwhelm these smaller cultural entities.

For a start, what is the cultural experience that binds us together? From the Atlantic to the Urals, as President de Gaulle used to tease us by saying, Europe has been characterised over many centuries by a broad unity of artistic experience. From Monteverdi to Haydn to Dvořák to Borodin to Debussy, to name but a handful, European composers have written to common rules of structure and harmony. Some of it is better than other, but the evolving language of music is universally taught, universally written down, and universally comprehensible across all linguistic barriers. It is playable and played by performers of any nationality, and heard and understood by every nation in Europe and most races under the sun. It is an extraordinary shared means of expression and communication.

Theatrically, the stage language and conventions of Chekhov or George Bernard Shaw or Schiller or Calderon are generally recognised and enjoyed. For centuries playwrights of all nations have drawn on the artistic tap-root that is Greek drama. The European novel embraces everything from Tolstoy, Dostoevsky, Flaubert, Cervantes, Thomas Mann and Jane Austen. Within that unity, there are important differences of sensibility and subject matter. No English writer could have written *Crime and Punishment*; no Russian writer would have cared to write *Sense and Sensibility*; no German author could have conceived of *Don Quixote*. All these authors reflect their nation, class and culture. Yet, their works are recognisably European, in the sense that the *Tale of Genji*, written by the Lady Murasaki in eleventh-century Japan, is not accessible, enthralling though it is.

In the case of music, the twentieth-century avant-garde takes its own national forms. Its well-spring was a single controversial one: the twelve-note serialism of the Second Viennese School of Webern, Berg and Schoenberg. Contemporary experimentalism draws from a wider range of sources. But the difference between the collagist Russian Alfred Schnittke and the jazz-influenced Briton Mark-Anthony Turnage, is more personal and stylistic rather than fundamental. Even minimalism – which some would see as an American creation – turns out to have many forms in different countries, with both Lithuania – in the person of Arvo Paart – and Britain – in the shape of John Tavener – producing composers of an ecstatic, religious, mystical bent, using many of the forms and tricks of minimalism. Arvo Paart is very popular in Britain; he is part of the European experience, the European musical identity. Tavener, though very English, writes music that is fundamentally shaped by his conversion to Greek Orthodoxy. His universality stems from his absorption of the very particular influences derived from another culture and religion.

Europe's composers use a common language and notation, which permit the widest range of individual style, local characteristics and national voices. They have a clear European identity within which they can express themselves in a variety of often extremely nationalistic and local forms. A good thing too: no one would want to listen to a Euro-composer, working to a compositional policy issued by the EU's Cultural Affairs Directorate – someone who might be defined as having the sense of fun of a German, the organisation of an Italian, the experimentalism of a Belgian, and the cosmic gloom of an Englishman. The strength of the European creative musical community derives precisely from its diversity of national and regional expression.

So, too, with musical performance. It is still possible to hear the distinctive and thrilling bray and rasp of Russian brass from the St Petersburg Philharmonic; the authentically woody tone of Czech clarinets; the deliberately tubby inflection of German horns. Each subtly indicates who you are listening to, each expresses a particular voice, perhaps even the national soul. Every orchestra plays the same notes, but the sense and sound, the shaping of phrase, the feeling for rhythm they communicate are distinctive, particular, local. Only Viennese players instinctively hold back the first beat in the bar of a waltz. Few non-French orchestras float the long lines of French melody as effortlessly as their nationals do. No one would have as their first choice an Italian orchestra playing Beethoven, Germans playing Rossini, or French playing Tchaikovsky. There is nothing chauvinistic in this; it merely reflects the joy of European variety,

like the delight to be had in the differences of European scenery
and the very different feelings each evokes. You can love both
the Lake District and the Alps, the Fens and the Po Valley, the
Loire and the Danube. Each is different but each is part of the
European landscape.

Yet precious though the diversity in musical performance may
be, it is increasingly at risk from homogenisation by the internal
and the international market. The analogy is with carrots or
potatoes in supermarkets. Customers, so supermarkets tell us,
demand vegetables of a convenient, nice, uniform shape and size,
not something twisted, odd, perhaps tasty and showing the
occasional blemish and crust of soil to prove they originated in a
garden. Yet customers – so supermarkets are reluctantly discovering – want taste, want variety, want fruit when it is in season.
The public's interest in difference rather than sameness is strong
and resilient and may be about to make itself truly felt in the
marketplace, whether vegetable or cultural.

In the musical supermarket, conductors are cosmopolitan and
peripatetic and may be upset by regional quiddity; recording
managers judge performances by their acceptability for an
international audience; orchestral players travel across national
boundaries and mix what they hear with what they instinctively
do. All are forces for bland homogenisation into a world identity,
a global style of playing, with the essential interest and the
character of the local sound in danger of being lost in the
process. Despite the existing differences noted above, who in a
blind test could honestly and immediately distinguish a British
from a Czech or an American orchestra playing Beethoven
today?

However, while these are powerful forces for harmonising the
musical experience (in the Brussels sense of 'harmonisation'), to
identify them and be anxious about them is not an argument for
sticking to wholly particularist expressions of cultural identity –
diving into the nearest minority bolt-hole and pretending the
global developments have gone away. For the forces of globalisation do not have to be forces for sterile uniformity; rather they

can produce even greater variety than the local scene could ever achieve by itself.

To be purely practical, the economics of artistic entrepreneurship demand the creation of multinational co-ventures made for performance at a series of arts festivals around the world. Peter Brook's innovative production of *Don Giovanni* at the Aix-en-Provence Festival in 1998 was seen in umpteen countries thereafter. The American minimalist Philip Glass's three-dimensional theatre piece *Monsters of Grace*, an attempt to define the nature of opera in the next century, was a co-production between ten festivals and theatres. The leading innovators on the international festival circuit – Robert Wilson, Robert Lepage, Peter Sellars – have to assemble international funding years in advance before creating the piece itself. Not for nothing are these ventures universally called 'projects'.

While such artistic confections carry their own dangers within them – dangers of preciosity, self-indulgence, a drive to the neurotically experimental – there is no doubt that such cross-breeding yields work that sticking to comfortable national spheres could not deliver. No single venue can mount such ambitious ventures by itself, and each tends to make a virtue of its financial need by deliberately seeking blends of international spice for its programmes.

More fundamentally, creators themselves increasingly want to cross cultural boundaries, to find inspiration in other traditions. For example: the American Philip Glass, in his misleadingly labelled 'opera' *Monsters of Grace*, combined state-of-the-art computer-generated, three-dimensional images with settings of poems by a thirteenth-century Persian mystic, Jelaluddin Rumi. This work defies definition, by genre or by music. Its very freedom from national categories makes it available as a source of experimentation from which all can learn – from both its successes and its failures – and develop.

There are other cases of this trend to hand. The Chinese-American composer Tan Dun has set the words of a sixteenth-century Chinese opera, *Peony Pavilion*, and counterpointed them with a tale of modern love in a production by the radical

American director Peter Sellars. The Romanian director Sylviu Purcarete has adapted and reinterpreted the ancient Greek *Oresteia* in twentieth-century terms. The Japanese director Yukio Ninagawa has created a version of *Hamlet* which is set in a Japanese theatre and uses occasional Kabuki techniques, but which tells one more about sixteenth-century English thinking and politics than any recent home-grown production. Again, seven contemporary American playwrights recently reset the emotions, loves and spirit of Shakespeare's sonnets in playlets about present American social and sexual tensions. Grounded though they were in the original text, they flew beyond it to intensify one's awareness of the timeless human understanding captured by the sonnets themselves.

The lesson is clear. These national artists are all looking to universal themes and inspirations for their own work, while remaining recognisably American, Japanese or Romanian in their basic approach. They are not offering a homogenised version of theatre which anyone can understand because the differences have been ironed out. Rather, they show how strong individual creation can be when it is rooted in strong, national terms of reference and blends them with international influences.

Conversely, there is an alternative contemporary trend in the arts world which celebrates the local by presenting it to an international audience. It is almost obligatory for any festival worthy of the name to draw inspiration from, or to take note of, ethnic artistic performance from around the world. The 1998 City of London Festival included performances by Australian Aborigines, Trinidadian steel bands, Southern Indian temple-dancers, Canadian Inuit throat singers.

This presents a teasing paradox. All these groups represent utterly distinct ethnic, racial or community cultures. As such they are lauded, admired and held up as worthy of study and even imitation. It is precisely because they are not part of mainstream European culture that we are invited to listen to them, respect what they exemplify and enjoy what they have to offer. Implicitly, they are also offered as a rebuke to the weight, authority, unity and consistency of the European artistic canon.

Should we apologise for our shared European inheritance, for its sheer quantity, its historical venerability, its dazzling variety and creativity? To do so would be preposterous, unnecessary and unwise. Not least, the very existence of this unquestionable European experience should form an essential counterpoint to the current political turmoil in the former Eastern Bloc, where the drive to ever smaller national and political units, and the attendant rancour and bloodshed, is one of the greatest threats to post-communist European stability.

What can creative culture offer to the continent that nurtured it? What can it contribute by way of analgesic in the messy course of giving birth to new European identities? I believe that there are at least four areas which will repay observation and could illumine the otherwise cheerless legal, institutional and political mechanics of European integration.

For a start, a culture as broad and historically deep-seated as the common European one cannot lurk in the ethnic or community particularism described above. True, folk-song has inspired composers as great and fertile as Kodály and Bartók and Stravinsky; true it provides recognition, reassures with familiarity and gives pleasure. Yet today's composers find inspiration in the great world outside as much as in local tradition. So do audiences. Europe has gone beyond mere folksiness, it is too mature and complex a civilisation to take refuge in such naive simplicities. Having said this, any culture that ignores its local origins totally loses part of its basic self.

For the process is a two-way one. Local cultures deserve and have their place; they must not be trampled on. They are like biological species whose massive diversity underpins the ecosystem. Many are prone to destruction by globalisation and seem too weak in the European experience to survive. We suppress them at our peril and to our loss, though how they can be strengthened naturally rather than artificially remains a problem. The experience of Irish governments in trying to preserve the Gaeltacht in its language and traditional way of life suggests that the job is just as difficult as breeding pandas in captivity.

But the contribution of culture spreads even further. National cultures have a huge political significance and a proven track record of being more effective at preserving democracy and democratic freedoms than political institutions devised for the purpose. Stalin could ignore legal or constitutional restraints and send political elites to the firing squad or the gulag and did so with devastating effect. He could terrify Shostakovich but could still not stop him writing music that serves as a blistering commentary on the dictator and all his works. Soviet despots could keep an iron grip on the media and the book trade; they could not stem the flow of samizdat publication by dissident writers or the outpouring of new novels and poems recited in a million kitchens throughout their empire. The KGB could consign their victims to remote Siberian exile; they had no control over the only exile that mattered, the 'internal exile' of the mind into which Soviet dissidents migrated, and where ideological thought-control had no dominion.

The political suppression of national cultures was a more stubborn problem. The Leninist-Stalinist policy towards the irksome nationalities that made up the Soviet Union was to authorise them in carefully sanitised forms, in what became discredited as 'folkloristic manifestations'. Here, every maiden and her partner existed in a world of fixed smiles, swirling ethnic, multi-petticoated skirts, stamping boots, relentlessly cheerful rhythms and rigidly restricted forms of innovation. This culture was not an expression of national identity; it was a fake substitute for it. It bought the regime some time but it gained no consent.

Ultimately, true national self-expression had the last word over the bogus Stalinist version. Let that be a warning to anyone who thinks that a huge and complex political unit (such as the Soviet Union was or the European Union is today) can have an 'official' unified culture. For genuine autonomous cultures are an essential safety valve for some, though not all, of the tensions that exist in all large units. In pre-1989 Poland, it was the cultural and religious independence of the Roman Catholic Church that acted as the core of resistance to the illegitimacy of Polish communist rule. Once the Party had to concede to the

Church a dual role in the social existence of the country, they had in effect lost the political and intellectual battle for minds.

In Czechoslovakia, the cultural resistance was more oblique but ultimately just as effective over time. It took the form of irony, self-deprecation and a typically Schwejkian form of stubborn, apparently uncomprehending resistance to authority. The satirising of lumpen communist dictatorship, the constant laughter behind a million backs, finally eroded the regime. The communists could suppress the Prague Spring of 1968, could send history professors to stoke boilers, journalists to clean windows, academics to man flower-stalls, but they could not stop the sly subversion of ridicule. Ridicule of the pretensions of an oppressive rule sprang from the character and tradition of the Czech people. It was expressed in the films, plays and novels of the national culture and – by a suitably ironic twist – the lampooned authorities did not seem to notice.

During the 1998 Prague Seminar on evolving European consciousness, it steadily dawned on British participants in the group devoted to culture that defining identity and according the proper role to local and national expressions had become a British as well as a European concern. Almost as much time was spent on the cultural experience of Scotland as on that of Serbia. If this seemed at first odd and was certainly unexpected, the analysis of the 'Scottish Question' was instructive. It went like this. For 250 years after the Union, and culminating in the Thatcher years, Scotland was not only subordinated to England politically but culturally as well. You do not have to be a card-carrying member of the SNP to recognise a certain truth in the perception that Scottish 'culture' had been virtually Leninised – that is to say reduced to a few token, vestigial symbols such as bagpipes, tartan, shortbread, haggis, whisky, a folksy accent and the bacchanalian celebrations of Hogmanay. It is undoubtedly the case that many Scots were happy to collaborate in the process.

No matter that during this same period Glasgow enjoyed a rebirth as 'Glasgow – City of Culture', or that the Glasgow School of painting flowered, the Scottish Colourists were rediscovered and Charles Rennie Mackintosh was re-appreciated. The continuing status granted by England to Scottish national culture was a subordinate, merely cute, one. But as with Czechoslovakia, there was a rebellious strain of an authentic Scottish identity which was alienated from Thatcherite London and later contributed to the sudden sweep towards the idea of self-government, and possibly even independence.

Yet, if Scotland is finding a way out of enforced inferiority and towards a new self-definition, this leaves a new problem of national delineation within Europe: Who are the English? What is Englishness? For years the English have imposed 'Britishness' on the component parts of the United Kingdom. Yet they also inflicted it on themselves. The English were rightly rebuked in no uncertain terms for using 'English' as if it were the most important component of 'Britishness'. For the Scots, Welsh and Irish, it was possible to be a nation and 'British' as well. But the price for their accepting Britishness was only tolerable if the English themselves, and alone within the United Kingdom, turned their back on their own particular national identity. The resulting paradox was that the 'English' could only be 'British'. They have been long bereft of legitimate, respectable ways of reflecting an English identity. The Cross of St George has been captured as an emblem of English nationhood by the least attractive, most violent and chauvinistic parts of the football-hooligan Far-Right. This leaves the task of recapturing ideas and the symbols of Englishness for England as a major task. A nation that has no clear cultural identity will also find the definition of its political nature very hard.

But there is a further lesson for all European cultures, whether they represent the voices of a region or nation, or the greater chorus of the whole European experience. All need to beware of a fake internationalism – that of the commercially branded global multi-nationals whose only interest is to eliminate differences. These seek to produce common products, uniform brands, and a unified corporate culture that springs neither from local experience, political background nor from artistic cross-fertilisation, but solely from the market-analysed reductionism of pecuniary opportunism. You cannot build any sort of identity on such a basis; nor is it intended that you should. For the merchants of this globalisation – who in certain manifestations include the 'harmonising' bureaucrats of Brussels – local diversity is an inconvenient obstacle to the most efficient manufacture and distribution of a series of universal, homogenised products. Their advocates and salesmen peddle a one-taste culture, one-style clothes, one-type organisation. This is not what Europe has created; this is not what Europe needs; this is not a solution for Europe's cultural and political problems.

Yet it is not as easy as that. You cannot saddle the multi-nationals with all the blame. We their customers must take our share. In the first flush of post-communist nationalism, the outward and visible signs of Western, internationalist consump-tion were potent and even revolutionary. Jeans, trainers, blousons and burgers marked the transition from Communist-Party-directed orthodoxy to apparent freedom, and above all to freedom of choice in what people bought. (The fact that these consumer goodies were also components of a commercially directed orthodoxy was less important for the time being.) The politics of plenty after a generation of the economics of restriction was heady. The challenge in these countries as they try to catch up with the huge head start of Western European prosperity is whether they can move from the customs of consumption to the culture of creation.

The task for European culture is to admit to itself that rock and pop music, video and advertising culture, trainers and jeans have given post-communist youth a set of cultural symbols more attractive, persuasive and conducive to unity than anything created on the continent in the last two millennia. Eurocrats for their part have to concede that political allegiance to a new undivided land mass has come not through indoctrination into the political and legal values of the institutions of Brussels but to the icons of international consumerism. For both – Europe's culture and its institutions – this is a hard message.

If there is a lesson be learned, it is that Europe needs a hierarchy of cultural identities, founded in regional or local expression, growing into national forms which are increasingly self-confident in their own work and which draw freely and richly from a wide range of international influences. This would represent a position of such strength that Europe's cultures could foster local variety of cultural growths and keep at bay the pseudo-globalising forces that speak of culture and identity but want only the standard and the homogeneous. Then, the burgers and the blousons can take their place as the mere decoration on a fundamentally European cake.

4 Culture, Society, Entertainment – Where is the Space for Art?

A cursory glance at the newspaper headlines proves one thing without a second look: no arts institution is easy to run. It was Ray Gunter, the Minister for Labour in Harold Wilson's 1964 Government, who described his job dealing with unemployment, wages and the trade unions as a 'bed of nails'. Getting off the arts world's spiky bed to confront fundamentals such as the place of art in society is overwhelmingly attractive. The bleared managerial eyes can lift from the computer screen, the mind detach itself from the uncertain horizons of a five-year plan based on annual funding, spreadsheets can be folded away, strategic targets set aside, the setting and fulfilment of objectives put off to a wet day, the congruence of Objectives with the Mission Statement temporarily shelved. From time to time it is useful – no, necessary – to ask the only questions worth addressing. What are the arts for? Where do they take their place alongside society's other preoccupations? We ought occasionally to test the arts against ideas of culture, society and entertainment in order to judge what their standing is and what their role should be.

Of course, we are already in the area of demarcation disputes – more stabs of pain to make Ray Gunter groan. For some people, the arts are coterminous with culture – indeed, a culture without arts could be said to be no sort of culture at all. The arts are an essential, perhaps defining, ingredient of any society worth the name – again, if a society has no culture what kind of society is it? And if the arts do not entertain, as well as all the other things expected of them, their fate will be a sad and speedy one. If this is right, then the very idea of implied contradictions may be bogus.

There are no tidy demarcations here. Are not the overlaps between the categories rather greater than the distinctions?

It is precisely because these terms part company at all that it is a valuable exercise to disentangle them further, to examine them as if they really were separate concepts. This is not just a game. I believe that the differences between culture, society, entertainment and the arts are real and growing larger and that we have to take the signs of this parting of the ways seriously.

To begin with, the perception of culture has become so broad, so inclusive that the word no longer belongs to the arts alone and cannot be monopolised by them. Ideas of society and community have grown more complex and qualified, too. Just as ethnic and social diversity has splintered the old simplicities of the socio-economic class system, so the arts no longer fit clearly into most of the definitions. As for entertainment, well this is the age, the generation of global, mass, instant and perpetual entertainment. That world could – and does – exist without any reference to the arts beyond the occasional act of cultural pillage and exploitation presented as an act of obeisance. (Slap a bit of Dvořák's *New World* symphony onto the bread advert to raise the tone of the commercial break; elevate televised football by prefacing it with Puccini or Fauré; tack Strauss's *Also Sprach Zarathustra* on any project or product where you want a vaguely futuristic feel.)

In short, I hear the sound of tearing of old connections between ideas that were once close, even automatic, partners. If I am right, then there is real cause for concern about the arts and their links with culture, society and entertainment. How long before the arts have to reply to Eliza Doolittle's defiant song of independence from Professor Higgins in *My Fair Lady*: 'I can do bloody well without you!'

Let me start with two personal vignettes. It is a January morning not so long ago and I am reading the papers over breakfast – newsprint as much as marmalade being an essential ingredient of morning digestion. A great many column inches are devoted to a new survey, 'British Lifestyles', on how we live today, what we enjoy, what we spend money on and so on.

Reading about how others spend their money is always fascinating. The survey has a deadly sting in the tail, just the single observation: 'In general the British public has little time for the arts.'

Second vignette. I am browsing through W. H. Smith at Heathrow to see if any half-way-respectable novels catch the eye for airline reading. At one end of the shop, the label 'Lifestyle' heads a whole racked wall of magazines. On closer inspection, every one of them is devoted to some aspect of sex. Now, I do not want to pretend to a naïveté that I do not have, but I had thought that at least some of the lifestyle section might be about something else – motorcars, gardening, clothes, wine, CDs. No, there was just cover after cover of sex and its overwhelmingly laddish indulgence and exploitation.

The second vignette momentarily explained the first. If the British public has little time for art, are they all spending their time indulging in 'lifestyle' between consenting adults? Can things be as bleak as that? Not necessarily. There are other cases of random, anecdotal evidence which point in the opposite direction and to more hopeful conclusions.

Several pieces of news suggest the sheer practical usefulness that the arts have beyond their usual boundaries. A regional rail operator started playing Delius – precise works unspecified – over the loudspeakers on a station's platforms in an attempt to cheer the place up. Lo and behold, the crime rate at that railway station dropped significantly. The mind boggles. Was Delius so soporific that he simply bored vandals out of lawlessness? Is he uniquely the most effective at soothing the savage delinquent breast? Field trials should be held to determine whether other composers restore law and order even more dramatically.

In education, the evidence is stacking up that teaching of the arts produces huge benefits to the whole of the learning process. A research study in 1993 established that listening to Mozart boosted IQ scores in intelligence tests and enhanced students' spatial reasoning performance. Another test demonstrated that taking part in art and drama activities led to significant improvement in the quality, range and imagination of students' writing. One 1997 project showed that pupils who learned the piano performed better in mathematics computation; while another study in the same year found that a positive mood-change among disturbed children was produced by playing them music as part of the daily routine.

A more surprising instance of the power of music came from abroad. Turkish police authorities have attempted to stop their ferocious riot police from being, well, quite so ferocious. As part of their state-of-the-art riot suppression gear, the new helmets contain internal transceivers through which the policemen hear their orders. But they receive more than mere orders. As the troops wait, tense, poised for perhaps bloody confrontation, Mozart and Beethoven will be fed into their minds in order to restrain their violent impulses. The Turkish police authorities must have calculated that Western music inspired by Turkish martial influences – like Mozart's *Rondo alla Turca*, or his *Seraglio* Overture – might be counter-productive, being both nationalist and unduly reminiscent of the warlike tones of the Janissaries' Band. No doubt Beethoven's military set-piece *Wellington's Victory*, where British and French armies clash musically, should be off the police's play-list too. Beyond that, the field is wonderfully open, with Beethoven's *Moonlight* Sonata at the top of the list as likely to slow heartbeats and reduce stress symptoms.

Back home, Sunderland Football Club adopted the march from Prokofiev's *Romeo and Juliet* ballet music as its theme for the team's march onto the pitch at the beginning of the match. The club also programmes classical dance performances with orchestra during the half-time break. The vigour of the Prokofiev march is said to disconcert visiting teams by its assertiveness, far less blatant and purely confrontational than the All Blacks' pre-match 'Hakka', and the football crowd loves the classical ballet.

Not to be left out, another football club has advanced straight into the heartland of arts sponsorship. Entering the Royal Academy in London for the English Regional Art Treasures exhibition in 1997, the sponsors' boards proclaimed that the exhibition's unlikely backers were Peterborough United. Their motto: 'Where Football and Art Meet'. If that slogan has a deliberately unresolved air to it – is Peterborough's football as good as art? Does art feature in the ground and the club? – it offers a teasing mix. Something is going on; some curious, tentative, limited synthesis between art and the rest of culture, a recognition that art is not quite so remote from daily occupations as it is accused of being, something very much more than tarting up commerce with a layer of artistic cosmetic.

None of that, however, solves the problems or removes my anxieties about the threats to the arts. We must return to those tiresome and tricky definitions and distinctions set out at the beginning. As in showjumping, the only way to take a series of difficult jumps is to carry them in one great flowing swing without hesitation.

Thus: 'Culture' includes all the ways in which we think and behave.

'Society' consists of the structures in which our behaviours are regulated and controlled.

'Entertainment' embraces all the ways in which we spend time when we are not working for a living.

The 'Arts' represent all those creative activities which are distinct from the other three but which attempt to make sense and meaning out of them.

If those definitions are correct, then they contain a danger by seeming to push the arts to the periphery; the others can get along perfectly well without them. More, the activities embraced by culture, society and entertainment are now so varied, available and engrossing that the time or inclination to devote time or money to the arts is declining. Has society got other, better, easier things to do?

At first glance, a rich, developed, consumer society such as Britain has never had so many diversions available to it. Leaving aside the desperate experience of enforced unemployment, actual free time, the precious hours not spent working for a basic living, has been transformed into leisure. Leisure has become an industry, and a growth industry at that.

Take home-listening to music. In 1985, only 2% of households had CD players. By 1995, the proportion had risen to 56% and is

still higher today. Over the same period, CD sales have rocketed.
In 1981, a miserable 3.1 million were sold; in 1993, the number
stood at 93 million a year. A break-down of those sales by music
categories reveals that two-thirds of the total were of rock and
pop. Only 7% of CD purchases were of classical music and a mere
2% were of jazz. Contrary to popular assumptions, jazz lovers are
a very select minority, and – numerically at least – not
particularly significant. They are, however, very vocal, very
knowledgeable and very persistent in demanding attention for
their type of music.

Since those figures were compiled, by the middle of 1998 the
classical CD market had taken a further down-turn with its
supposedly 'classical' lists increasingly padded with compilations,
easy listening, mood transformers and pop crossover artists.

The video recorder has also won its place by the hearth. By
1995, 80% of UK households had a VCR but demand for them
was still not satisfied. Sales of VCRs hit a new record in that
year, with no fewer than 25% of homes owning two or more
machines, many of them presumably of the latest model.

What do people use them for? In 1986, the value of the video-
rental market was seven times larger than that for buying videos.
By 1992, the value of bought videos was running neck and neck
with the value of rented ones. By 1995, the video purchase
market was 50% larger than the rental market. At about the
same time, those households that bought videos had on average
26 pre-recorded tapes in their possession. (No doubt most of
those were destined to wither unseen, a reproach and a reminder
of all the good programmes we should have watched!)

What videos did customers buy? In the all-time Top-Twenty
list of bought videos, the top seven are all Disney productions.
The Jungle Book heads the sales list and *Bambi* romps in at
number seven. Not a lot of art there. We should marvel at the
unerring instinct of Walt Disney for creating a well-nigh
universal set of myths of reassurance. Certainly, the demand for
them appears to be virtually limitless. Should we concede
without demur such a tyranny over taste and understanding,
however voluntarily accepted?

CDs and videos are for private home consumption. The home, especially the satellite-driven one, is the most available entertainment centre. But audiences are increasingly going out for their entertainment. While cinema-going will never return to the heady days of the 1960s, its revival in the 1990s and the upswing in British film production have been much noticed and lauded features of the present cultural/artistic scene. Film-making is hailed as one of the 'creative industries' by which the newly re-branded Britain is identified and from which it will flourish. The number of cinema screens doubled in the decade from 1985 to 1996, and annual attendances increased by 45 million or some sixty per cent during the same period. No self-respecting commercial centre or shopping mall is complete without its multiplex, offering a choice of films undreamed of in the post-war heyday of film-going. At that time, peace was the rarity, rationing a normality, every film ran for a week at the local, every programme had a 'B' feature and the idea of choice was an undemanded luxury.

The range of available pastimes does not end there. By the middle of this decade, the number of homes with satellite TV had grown to fourteen per cent of the total; the numbers subscribing to cable systems was rising fast but from a very low base. Yet in the TV viewing world, an interesting phenomenon is discernible. As the number of channels increases overall, as the total amount of viewable material grows exponentially, the total time actually spent in viewing any television falls.

In the three years up to 1995, viewing had fallen by some ten per cent in those homes with access to satellite and cable – that is to say, homes with the highest volume of television material to choose from watched less. What will be the impact of the much-hyped new digital revolution, releasing hundreds of channels onto a public mainly still content with five plus a video recorder? Is the audience really yearning for choice in terms of greatly increased numbers of channels? Or will the digital operators be denied the bonanza they hope for and need? All we know at present is that increased supply does not appear to stimulate demand. The reason may be that quality determines viewing rather than quantity, and no amount of mouthing of the word 'choice' means anything unless it is associated with better programming. There is a warning for the arts there.

Taking all these trends together, there have never been more alternative calls on people's time, leisure and money than there are today. Most are easier to enjoy than the activities offered by the arts. Most are far cheaper, especially satellite television, although even there price is a deterrent to subscription. Most of today's diversions are far more convenient, do not involve a journey, do not demand prior booking and some are available at the flick of a remote control. Most of them set out to entertain as part of their basic assumption. Most of them seek to find out what has pleased the audience in the past and then try to repeat that known success. By contrast, the permanent commitment of the arts to innovate, to challenge, to unsettle, even to disturb, sets them at a distance from the other available diversions. By definition, by choice, by their very nature, they are on something of a loser in today's 'easy-please' social circumstances.

It is not therefore surprising that the statistics for the way we use the arts in all their shapes and forms present a more complex, more confused picture than those for the worlds of entertainment. Some aspects are encouraging. In each year during the decade up to 1994, no less than 25% of the adult population said they had gone to the theatre. This would create a core play-going audience of some 9 million. If that looks momentarily reassuring for the arts, consider the composition of these 9 million theatre visits. Most are to musicals, closely followed by children's plays and the annual, seasonal rite of the pantomime. Remove those three categories and the audience left for classical or contemporary theatre is remarkably small.

Or consider the audiences for live classical music, an activity less popular than going to the cinema or visiting the betting shop. In a recent survey, 33% of respondents said they had been to the cinema in the previous three months; 19% had been to a museum – Sunday afternoon museum-going has replaced the weekly visit to church for many. Just 8% – a low figure, you may think – had been to a pop concert and 7% to a classical concert.

If that 7% appears hearteningly large, further analysis suggested that only two-thirds of that number were truly committed classical music attenders, representing at best a gross number of some $3\frac{1}{4}$ million people. They are certainly a small minority. Yet, according to the Association of British Orchestras, 'there are more people going to concerts! New Halls in Birmingham, Manchester and elsewhere have seen huge surges in audiences, and we have in the BBC Proms the world's best attended and most successful festival of orchestral music.' A true observation so far as it goes, but the financial indebtedness of many British orchestras points to an arts sector with more than its share of problems.

With all statistics, and impressions, interpretation is important. Raw numbers are not to be taken at face value, nor does the single snapshot figure tell the whole story. Look at the longer trends. For instance, the audience for opera has grown by a quarter in the last eight years. It is immeasurably larger than it was fifty years ago when a permanent British opera company, not to mention two national companies and three regional companies, could only have been an opera fanatic's dream. Audiences for ballet and dance have expanded too, given the increased supply and availability of national and international touring companies. As the Association of British Orchestras pointed out, there are more orchestras now than there were fifty years ago; more children studying music; more engagement between musicians and children in schools themselves.

Encouraging as those observations are, it is still impossible to escape the conclusion that – statistically at least – the arts are firmly on society's sidelines. According to 'British Lifestyles', the amount we spend on holidays and entertainment has increased by eleven per cent in the last decade. But once spending on the Lottery, cinema-going, health and fitness clubs and bowling alleys is removed – 'lifestyle' spending if ever there was – most of that increase has been accounted for. The arts do not feature as a prime call on money available for most people's discretionary spending. The evidence from every arts venue is that audiences have to watch their budgets, are very sensitive to price increases,

have eagle eyes for bargain subscription offers, do not wine and
dine regularly or lavishly as part of their evening out, and choose
carefully when and where to spend their hard-earned pounds. For
those with money to spend, the preferred venue for a good night
out is not a concert hall, a theatre or an art gallery. It is a newly-
built, all-purpose, multi-entertainment leisure centre.

Yet before we descend into terminal despair, other, more
cheering, pieces of evidence must be put into the balance. For
instance, in an Arts Council survey, half the public say they
'personally value' having arts events and facilities in their
neighbourhood. A majority agree with the proposition that 'arts
have a beneficial impact on the area they live in'. More than half
say that the arts improve the local quality of life. Just over two-
thirds judge that the arts keep town centres lively and make
them more attractive to visit. These are 'soft', unquantifiable
indicators; they will not sell tickets or fund theatre companies.
Yet they are clear, valuable and positive perceptions.

Nor are they just British perceptions. Recently, the City of
Amsterdam commissioned a study of the social and economic
significance of the professional arts for Amsterdam. It found that
the arts contribute significantly to the regional economy; that
they create jobs; that part of Amsterdam's overall character and
appeal for visitors of all kinds is defined by its arts. The economic
justification is solid.

Yet, the survey's most important findings related to how the
arts make people feel. While 87% said they were 'proud' of
Amsterdam's cultural activities, no fewer than 89% said they 'felt
good' after visiting a given form of art. And 60% said that such
attendance contributed to the development of their knowledge
and taste. Those are very appreciative reactions. Why have the
arts not been able to gain credit for creating this level of approval
and gratitude at the social and personal level? If a national-well-
being index means anything, it should include room for such
indicators.

In the United States, the arts community has delved thoroughly into the reasons for failing to transmit a sense of the value
of the national culture. In Britain, we are too often bogged down

in debilitating anxieties and rows about national and local funding. The Americans have identified explicitly what we acknowledge almost regretfully or apologetically: namely that there is a tussle between private gains and public responsibility, most clearly evident in the world of culture and the arts. Because Americans live in a totally profit-oriented culture, they are far more clear-headed than Britons about the role and value of what they call simply the 'not-for-profit' sector. For the tension between the two sectors can be a creative one.

For Americans of all stripes, the not-for-profit sector is an essential and honourable part of the social environment. In a profit-driven society it is no cause for shame that some activities do not make money. It is recognised as an intrinsic part of their nature. And as a good citizen, it is part of one's civic responsibility to overcome the shortfall as best as one can. Most active American business leaders devote a significant part of their lives and time to working for a 'not-for-profit'. Over there, no one has to apologise for doing so or for actively soliciting support for their pet project; it is expected and recognised as right. Here we are blamed for constantly holding out the begging bowl, because the arts are classed as 'charities', a word with almost irredeemably Victorian overtones of indigence and failure to stand on one's own feet.

Yet even the use of the wholly respectable American category of not-for-profit does not remove all tensions from the country where it was invented. In a major survey of the US arts scene by the National Endowment for the Arts, an American theatre director expressed deep worries that everybody in the British arts world will recognise. 'What all of this debate is about', he observed, 'is driving the not-for-profit culture into the market-place, so that there are no distinctions, so that all of our ideas are shaped by the marketplace. We need enclaves where ideas are not driven by capital, we need not-for-profit enclaves where ideas emerge for other purposes than the advancement of capital.' Those safe havens are concert halls, libraries, museums, galleries, theatres, anywhere that the main activity cannot be quantified, places which flout the increasingly omnipresent orthodoxy that only quantification can truly legitimise anything.

Over the last decade, the arts in Britain have been called on to justify themselves by a whole new series of criteria: they should be efficient and economical; should regenerate the neighbourhood, contribute to employment and wealth creation; should teach by bringing arts into schools and heal by working in hospitals; comfort the elderly, overcome racial disharmony, lower social barriers, alienate no one, cater for the disabled, and meet masses of requirements only recently dreamed up, and by people without knowledge of the arts or experience of them.

The one principle never put at the head of such externally imposed demands is that the art itself should be excellent – creative, innovative and amazing. What a back-to-front set of priorities! Worse, the arts have gained little credit in society's eyes even as they have successfully met the burdensome new objectives laid upon them.

It is no comfort that the Americans have had the identical experience. As one arts centre director complained, though sadly – and typically – in opaque managerial language: 'As we ever more effectively demonstrate our ability to forge synergistic links with diverse and multiple constituencies, often adding considerably to our budgetary commitments, both public and private support for arts institutions is on the decline.' Translated into English: 'As we cope more and more with the external tasks thrust upon us, we get less and less money for our pains from both public and private sources.'

So what must the arts do to earn society's recognition and keep up with the other competitors for our audience's attention? They must be more robust in insisting on management language, terms and prescriptions that are suited to the world of arts. They must harness the new media to their cause. The more CD-ROMs there are about musicians, dancers, writers, painters or museums, the greater the intellectual community of those who share in their irreplaceable and infinitely precious creation. The more the Internet contains information about and knowledge of the arts, the more they will become an essential and inescapable part of its influences and values. Of course, for some people, the screen will be a sufficient point of access to the arts; it will never lead them to a concert or museum. But overall, the CD-ROM will contribute to a greater critical mass of awareness and understanding of the arts than we have now.

In today's world, the arts depend on television and have been deeply damaged by mainstream television's migration from arts coverage as a regular part of television culture. The principal TV stations must show more arts performances and discussions about them on their main channels. The opportunity to use new digital channels as showcases for the best in British live arts creation is a historic one. More operas, concerts, dance and plays – sometimes live, sometimes recorded – would make them routinely accessible. In this way, the arts can reassert their value and become reintegrated into the broader stream of culture as a way of life. Yet the digital route is also a dead end; if the arts are marginalised, turned into a ghetto for the converted, the idea of the arts as a mainstream part of life will never be made. Terrestrial television cannot meet its responsibilities to art by shunting it off into a digital siding.

The arts should hold candid discussions with society in schools, homes, high streets about where and why they part company. They must be honest about facing charges – however unfair they may feel or may be – about being remote, exclusive, irrelevant and incomprehensible. Society must be equally honest in answering charges that it is materialistic, indifferent, superficial and shallow. At the end of such a dialogue, society and the arts may have narrowed the gap between them.

Finally, the arts should rediscover a sense of fun, of light-heartedness, of the joys of diversion. Perhaps there are things to be learned from the sheer professionalism of the worlds of entertainment. I do not believe that the arts singly or collectively live in a Malvolio world where we begrudge anyone the enjoyment of their cakes and ale. Besides the arts should not surrender the vocation of being entertaining so easily to others. They should try to sit more comfortably than they sometimes seem to do with the very idea of entertainment rather than squatting grouchily outside the circus tent.

But equally there are things that the arts must not do. They must never cease to be true to themselves; nor pretend to be easier than they need to be; nor capitulate to anyone who says they are too difficult. They must not be frightened of stating that real rewards require effort from audiences and participants. They should not behave as if they are ashamed of their past or as if their pride in it prevents them from belonging to the future. They must not be coy about what makes them different. Especially in the marketplace of life, they must not sell themselves short.

If they stay true to what they are, but accept the challenge of constructive engagement with their critics, then we could see the arts again interlocked with culture, society and entertainment in a way that satisfies us all.

5 The Good Society – Can You Get It On the Cheap?

It was almost fifty years ago that a group of students at the London School of Economics began to mull over their ideal of what constituted the 'Good Society'. It was a very post-war thing to do. Nazism and Fascism had been defeated. Despite the immediate problems of economic recovery in a European continent devastated by war, things could only get better. True, the Soviet Union was behaving less like the great wartime coalition partner against Hitlerite Germany, more like a state and ideology with its own, alarming agenda. Shouldering these anxieties, it was right for bright, hopeful young men to gather from time to time to think about the grand scheme of things and what could be brighter or grander than contemplating the 'Good Society'?

Forty years later, one member of the 1949 Seminar Group, the philosopher Alan Milne, posed a set of questions relating to the topic and suggested to his friends that they should invite a speaker to try to answer them once a year. John Burgh, one-time Director General of the British Council, subsequently President of Trinity College, Oxford, asked me to do so in 1996. After the customary feeling of regret that I had accepted another speaking engagement, especially one where real thought would be needed, I found that the invitation provided hours of innocent entertainment. It was not only when discussing the subject at home, but on those otherwise duty-led social occasions when a sudden silence was filled by my asking my dinner partner, 'How would you define the Good Society?' It is a well-nigh sure-fire conversation-stopper. The last time I tried it was at the Mansion House. When the look of dismay had left my neighbours' faces, two of them asked nervously how long I had to talk for. 'Ten minutes?' they enquired hopefully. No, I replied, 'more like three-quarters of an hour'. We turned to other, simpler matters.

At first, thinking about what makes a good society appeared attractively simple. All sorts of quick and easy stipulations leaped to mind. Creating a good society brings out the social dictator. For instance: it would be one where all personal counselling was banned on the grounds that it does more harm than good, because it is based on bastard and half-digested Freudianism and because it peddles the fantasy that well-meaning chat, deep 'concern' and a readiness to 'share', without any theoretical foundation to the process, can solve emotional problems.

A good society would have nothing to do with the so-called 'caring' professions. Indeed it would ban them. In their place, it would have the 'indifferent professions', that is to say those organisations who do good because it is their job to help and not because they confuse indulgence in mushy emotions with a professional task. I use the word 'indifferent' as in the translation of the instruction in the lavatories of old French railway trains: 'turn the tap indifferently to left or to right'. The tap works – but not because it cares either way. So would the 'indifferent' professions.

A good society would be one where eating while walking in the street – not to mention throwing away the container – would be banned on the grounds that it is fattening, polluting, and disgusting to look at. Casual eating is no better than casual sex. It damages social cohesion by reducing those occasions when people sit down, face to face, and enjoy a conversation. It trivialises the sacramental experience of breaking bread together. Banning promiscuous, impulse eating in public would help to increase the times that families talked and related to one another – or even learned to sulk in a sociable way – as a group.

A good society might consider banning TV zap-buttons on the grounds that they destroy the ability to concentrate and eliminate any possibility of viewers being stretched or surprised by a programme that catches them unawares before they have the time or energy to get off their couches and change the set manually. Or it might regulate 'flying Australian winemakers', on the grounds that replanting the world's marginal vineyards with millions of hectares of Chardonnay and flinging the result into oak barrels make the resulting vintage taste like toffee and flood the world with hectolitres of wine muzak. Or – well my list, like Gilbert's Lord High Executioner's, would be endless, and continuously updated.

But this was only a personal game. A truly good society could not be based on the impulses and prejudices of the individual, however satisfying that game might be. It certainly should not be founded on bans – hard cases make bad law and even worse social morality. It should offer general principles to which the majority can subscribe because more people will benefit than suffer from the results. Its laws and regulations would not be concerned with stopping people from doing things – the bad society is already far too adept at that – but with encouraging people to do things that are more attractive than the things we are tempted to stop.

But first, let me start with the questions that Alan Milne posed to get the lecture series started in the '90s. How do his own assumptions about a good society stand today, and how well or badly does contemporary Britain fare against them? He called for a society without gender or racial discrimination. With women still experiencing prejudice and unequal opportunities in the job market and with racial attacks in Britain running at the rate of tens of thousands each year, we can hardly feel that we have met his performance target. Yet we have surely moved to a 'Better' if not yet a 'Good' society. Thanks to equal opportunities policies at work and the Race Relations Act (however patchily they are implemented), those discriminated against now have some chance of redress and the more obnoxious forms of bigotry have been labelled as crimes. Is it too much to believe that institutional and legal restraints on behaviour are gradually, if painfully slowly, encouraging changes in perception and that good behaviour will finally drive out bad?

Alan Milne again: 'A good society cannot be indifferent to the plight of the poor, the unfortunate and the helpless in its midst.'

With an underclass of some ten per cent of the population; with more beggars and people sleeping rough in our cities; with hardly a street corner without its seller of the *Big Issue*; with the human experiments of so-called 'Care in the Community' wandering in a bemused way around the nation's streets; with clear proof that increased wealth at the top does not trickle down to the poor below, and the gap between rich and poor growing steadily, our society gives a passable imitation of indifference to the poor and helpless. If there is a social welfare safety net, then its holes seem to be getting ever bigger. We seem to have become deaf to the sounds of bodies falling through that net.

Finally, I can only quote with admiring sadness the sheer idealism of Alan Milne's final sentence: 'If all are to enjoy modest prosperity, some will have to forgo part of the greater prosperity they could otherwise have achieved.' *Sancta simplicitas*. It is now part of bipartisan economic and political orthodoxy that the middle and upper classes should not be taxed more highly than they are, that receiving an income of £100,000 a year is not to be considered rich, that enterprise culture demands an enterprise class whose rewards should be limitless and comparable with the greatest available anywhere on earth. In the early years of Thatcherism, a top tax rate of fifty per cent was regarded as perfectly acceptable, generous even. Today, under a New Labour government, the suggestion that this tax rate might be restored is held up as punitive on a Stafford Crippsian scale. If the pips are to be made to squeak, today's squeaking pips belong to the already poor. Who cares about modest prosperity for all? Outstanding riches for some seems a more accurate description of the society we have created. We have a long way to go to meet the criteria sketched out in this very decade for the lecture series.

Ideas for ways to take up the subject came at odd times and odd places. One night, we were reeling out of Covent Garden after *Das Rheingold*. There was John Burgh observing challengingly 'How about that as a theme for the "Good Society"?'

It certainly offers many instructive variations on the theme. Wotan builds Valhalla as a home for the gods and as a sign that he is ending the compulsive globe-trotting and philandering that so annoy his wife, Fricka. He is not the first or the last man to build an ideal home for his wife out of sexual guilt, but he remains as an awful warning to those who contemplate it. Like many conscience-stricken men, he does not have the money to pay for his guilt-nest. Wotan then makes two mistakes. First he mortgages a member of his family – Freia – to the builders. Then, knowing that he will forfeit his mortgage because he does not have the cash to repay it, he employs a shifty spiv called Loge to steal what is necessary to avoid the repo men, the giants Fafner and Fasolt, taking the property they have built. Of course, Alberich and Mime are loathsome dwarves who themselves want to dominate the world, but does that justify stealing the Rheingold from them by lying and trickery?

In all this, Wagner's sense of moral right and wrong is impeccable. His entire cycle is built on the proposition that those who choose absolute power will forfeit the possibility of love. The search for power, once tasted, becomes unquenchable and obsessive, leading to treachery, murder and death. Love can overcome the lust for power but only if it renounces and rejects power, as Brünnhilde does. For reasons unstated, only the Rhinemaidens can handle the source of all power without contamination. But, as the lustful Alberich complains, being slippery as eels perhaps they have no time or inclination or capacity for love as we know it.

Wagner, too, insists on the importance of legality. Wotan, that clear-eyed, but one-eyed god, tries to impose order on the world through a series of treaties and contracts, all recorded and inscribed on the ash staff that he carries with him. But Wotan betrays his own beliefs. 'The trouble with you', says Fricka, 'is that you don't stick to what you swear to.' Later, the dwarf, Alberich, asserts that Wotan is actually no better than he himself – a practitioner of Realpolitik, all too ready to break his word when it suits his ends.

In short, and nothing else about *The Ring* is short, Wagner presents a moral universe where power corrupts, love conquers, would-be universal rulers are destroyed by the contradictions involved in achieving their ambition, treaties are better kept than broken, and even the supposed hero is sufficiently gullible as to allow himself to be drugged and then to seduce his bride on behalf of someone else. No wonder they all come to a very wet and sticky end. And don't forget the first and also the final lesson: always pay your builders.

On reflection, I first thought about the good society at school, or rather a close and far cleverer friend did the thinking for me. A year older than I was, he kindly allowed me to sit at his feet as he put the world to rights. It was, he asserted, wrong that we young would have to live our mature lives in a world that had been shaped by decisions taken by the old. We were prevented from being responsible for our destinies. Those politicians or so-called statesmen who formed that world for us would not experience the consequences of their actions, for they would be long dead. Everyone should accept responsibility for making the beds of life on which they would have to lie.

'So, Socrates,' I dutifully put in when I could, 'how do we put right this unjust state of affairs?' Socrates obliged. If we were all to learn the moral principle that we must live with the consequences of our own actions, then the government of affairs in a country should be entrusted only to those between the ages of twenty-five and forty. Once we reached forty, we would be disqualified from government, and turn our attention to other matters – learning, the arts, religion, business, commerce or whatever took our fancy.

To objections that the young lacked the experience to govern wisely and well, the sage replied briskly that their abilities had never been tested, whereas if you wanted a monument to the achievements of the old you only had to look at the mess around you. He pushed his argument further: if there were indeed evidence that age and experience produced better government, the reward of learning early about responsibility and living with the consequences of one's actions would still be infinitely preferable.

There, amid the intellectual teasing, my precocious school friend hit on a serious truth: that we should all understand the connection between our acts and their outcomes and be accountable for them. These are crucial ingredients for making mature individuals as well as a good society. In the 1930s, the café entertainer Ronald Frankau, not renowned primarily as a moralist, had a song for it:

> You've got to pay for everything you get.
> It's a matter of considerable regret.
> Needless to repeat it,
> You can't have your cake and eat it,
> Sooner or later you'll have to pay the debt.

From the 1960s onwards, we elevated the business and language of rights above that of responsibilities. From human rights to women's rights, to children's rights to animal rights, the catalogue lengthened and became more sophisticated. It followed inexorably that rights – which were mere abstract aspirations without some weight behind them – required bolstering by being connected to entitlements, usually financial. Thirty years on, it is far from clear that the doctrines of rights have significantly advanced the cause of many of the championed categories, and it is abundantly clear that societies are reluctant or unable to pay the entitlements needed to turn claims into gains. Is it better or worse to deny rights by resisting them, to proclaim rights and then fail to realise them in practice, or to seek to gain a general advance through rights for all rather than pursue particular rights for special groups?

Recently, the public debate has shifted from rights to the seemingly more old-fashioned language of responsibilities. I do not believe that it is old-fashioned in the pejorative sense, but the way it is deployed sometimes has a backward-sounding ring to it. From errant fathers pursued by the Child Support Agency, to indifferent parents required to enter into a contract with their children's school, obligations will be codified, formalised and legalised. You will be told ('counselled' perhaps) how to be a good parent, a good single-parent, a good wife- or husband-to-be, a good ex-husband, and each life stage will have its own code of conduct, even its own charter. But will this new single-minded emphasis on responsibilities rather than rights achieve in its turn what is hoped for?

Some years ago, when Professor Charles Goodhart – now at the London School of Economics and a member of the powerful Bank of England Economic Monetary Policy Committee – was at the Bank of England, he coined a useful but inadequately noticed maxim. In the field of economic management, he observed, if a single economic indicator was elevated above others as the principal yardstick of the economy's performance, it usually became distorted and ultimately distorted the performance of the economy itself. A similar observation might apply to principles governing social and moral behaviour: to elevate rights alone, or to concentrate purely on responsibilities, invariably leads to imbalance or malformation. They cannot exist by themselves. Treating them in isolation warps the other factors with which they need to interact to make up a good society.

At Cambridge, I was taught medieval history by a great Austrian historian, Walter Ullmann. A lawyer by training, Ullmann applied the study of legal principles and terminology to the workings of the medieval Papacy. He seasoned his lectures with slightly puzzled, but always pointed, recollections of his time in the British Pioneer Corps during the war. Peopled as it was by politically 'unreliable' exiles such as Walter, the Pioneer Corps must have had the highest average IQ of any British military unit. One day, as the Sergeant Major ran his recruits ragged across the parade ground, Ullmann found himself reflecting on the institution to which he now belonged. Could it really be, as it seemed, one in which a few had unlimited powers and the majority, like himself, had none? Or was it not, surely, like a Roman 'corporatio'? If the latter, then any member must have duties, rights and privileges.

The Sergeant Major dismissed the parade – giving rise to another Ullmannism: 'You know, that is just like the priest who says at the end of the Mass, "Ite, missa est" ' – and Walter decided to make formal enquiries about the true nature of the army from the Company office. He marched in and asked where – since he knew all too much about his army duties – he should look for his rights and privileges. The Duty Corporal marched him back to his barracks so fast that his feet hardly touched the ground.

But Ullmann was right. Duties, rights and privileges are the essential legs of a moral, legal and political tripod. Putting all the weight on one to the exclusion of the others leads to bad laws, bad social practices and buckles the workings of society; omitting one causes it to topple over. Perhaps it is the very swing from rights to duties that causes the instability. Privileges, too, have to be earned, not assumed as a right in themselves. Privileges only accrue when rights and duties have established their own balance.

In Siegfried Lenz's 1960s novel *The German Lesson*, a young man sentenced to prison for stealing paintings is required by his remedial prison regime to look back at his upbringing and the family influences that might have led him to jail. He remembers the deep sense of duty by which his father, a local policeman in Germany in the 1930s and 1940s, worked. When the Ministry of Culture in Berlin ordered that a local artist (clearly based on the Expressionist Emil Nolde) should be banned from painting, the dutiful policeman not only delivered the instructions but zealously enforced them, ensuring the painter was punished when they were ignored, even though the man had been his friend since childhood. A compulsive sense of duty, of properly executing his official responsibilities, carried all before it, unmediated by any sense that in doing right by himself and by his office, he might be denying the rights of another human being. In this caricature of responsibility – better presented as blind obedience – the policeman was untroubled by conflict between responsibility to the state and the claims of old friendship.

The rebellious policeman's son, however, had his own sense of duty. It impelled him to protect the artist's paintings from destruction by his father by removing them. Was he preserving or stealing them? But even this initially defensible moral drive itself became distorted as the young man began to take anyone's pictures when he had mere premonitions that they might come under threat.

Society, a good society, cannot be constructed on the basis of a single criterion, a social variant on the kind of 'one-club economics' for which Chancellors of the Exchequer were often excoriated. Here too the choices before us are polarised as lying between the market and the community. (We were assured, of course, under Thatcherism that 'society does not exist'! Blairism has reinstated it.) For many years, the model of the free market has been held up as the unchallengeable, indeed moral, foundation on which a good society should be based. Markets allow freedom, swap information, generate innovation, stimulate economic activity, allow competition, motivate enterprise and are the best form of social activity devised by man.

Yet markets – real or theoretical – are not filled with plaster saints whose main aim is to meet the public's demands for the most innovative goods and the most reliable services at the lowest possible price. Markets are filled with people who want to corner them, with hucksters, con-men and opportunists. The traders talk loudly about choice as if choice alone was an unchallengeable moral good. As Adam Smith – but not the Adam Smith Institute – observed, the natural impulse of any group of businessmen when they gather together is to exploit the market to their benefit as much as to pour benefits on their customers. From Gordon Gekko to Michael Milken to Ivan Boesky to John Meriwether, the financial free market's 'Lords of the Universe' have behaved – and been taken at their own valuation – as if they had built the machine that made gold. Ben Jonson would have loved it.

The language of the market has now to influence, even to dominate, most human activities. Any organisation worth its salt is supposed to exist by an internal market – though the National Health Service is now recognised as being unsuitable for it. This means that each and any transaction must be costed and can only occur if a price is put upon it; this price must be the lowest available. Purist advocates of the system would rather the transaction was costed in theory and not used than that it should take place on an imperfect cost basis. Not knowing the price of a transaction is now the ultimate managerial – human, even –

crime. To those who say that any transaction is only justifiable if its cost is known, I offer the words of the prayer: 'To give and not to count the cost'! The most cherishable human transactions in a good society are precisely those that are not costed because those concerned believe that the spirit of such uncalculated giving is essential to making a good society work.

But even within the narrower confines of an organisation, to turn relationships into market transactions, to put a price on them, is to miss the point. It reduces co-operation between individuals and creates administrative and bureaucratic barriers; it sets a price on ideas; it destroys a sense of corporate community; it fragments a sense of corporate belonging; it dehumanises because it materialises the human traffic of feelings, of curiosity, the satisfactions of mutual working together.

There is a graphic example of this tendency from the BBC World Service. While I was Managing Director, consultants urged us to price the use of the Library and Information service on the grounds that it was costing a lot of money to run. Some members of staff, it was alleged, used it too much. What, I asked, did 'using it too much' mean? The answer was that some staff used it more than the average. Perhaps, I objected, that reflected their diligence, their professionalism, their dedication, their concern to maintain standards. Perhaps they should be encouraged to use it still more. Possibly, came the reply, but the Library and Information centre could be run more cheaply if fewer people used it. I retorted that since the whole standing and credibility of the World Service rested on its accuracy, what was the point of saving a few pounds on a central service if you then risked losing the only priceless asset the organisation possessed – its reputation? Such are the purblind lengths to which the disciples of cheapness are ready to go. It is the modern *trahison des clercs*.

Management consultants know that the really worthwhile activities cannot be priced; but because they are unwilling or unable to confer a value on them, they try to imprison them within the confines of a price bracket or deny their validity at all. You cannot have a newspaper or a World Service that is accurate ninety per cent of the time. Almost anything that it costs to deliver the final ten per cent of accuracy or excellence is not just good value for money but an essential expenditure without which all prior costs would be a waste of time and money. The last ten per cent of expenditure may well create the real value, the one that defies analysis.

Yet the pressure of such a reductive outlook is relentless. How cheaply can a service be provided? That has become the ultimate question of existence, the principal justification of any activity. In the land of the cost-driven, the lowest tenderer is king. Only later do you discover the real basis on which the tender was submitted and realise that many a cost reduction has a service reduction built into it. A good society would balance the current obsession with price by an added concern for quality. That would indeed add value to the process of buying the best products, accepting the best contracts, supplying the best services. If value is intrinsically unmeasurable, it is also simply priceless. Were all the acts and goods supplied by individuals and enlightened institutions for non-economic reasons to be costed out, they would represent an industry of billions of pounds whose true contribution to society would still remain incalculable.

I have no doubt that some management consultant would establish that trying to cost the uncostable involved a vast waste of public resources and should be adequately prioritised or stopped altogether. Alternatively, that such an activity was so economically important that it should immediately be scrutinised for value for money. Surely the Good Samaritan would have been well advised not to tarry by the wayside (even though Mrs Thatcher thought he could help because he could afford to). He should have stopped to calculate the opportunity cost of the time he might spend in helping the man set upon by thieves. He might decide that it was economically more efficient to hurry by on the other side, despatching a team of consultants to persuade the battered man of the dangers of becoming dependent on others.

Beyond threatening a sense of the truly valuable, the untrammelled market damages notions of a good society by challenging the very concept of the individual. In such forms of market differentiation, old-fashioned class and social background are replaced by categories such as 'Stylish Singles', 'Pebble-dash Subtopians', 'Rootless Renters', or 'Bijou Homemakers'. Such 'geo-demographic segmentation' is an essential marketing tool for anyone engaged in the business of selling. The titles may be facetious, but their purpose is serious: to sub-divide individuals into minute selling units, niches to be targeted in and by the market. No one would answer to being a member of the 'Suburban Mock Tudor' category, still less to being a denizen of the 'Bulldog Estates', though honesty might demand recognising oneself as 'Ageing Professional', 'Moneyed Emigré', or 'High-spending Grey'. In days gone by, all those would have fitted snugly and happily into a different sub-group: 'Corporate Careerists'. Whichever title is given, in the world of the market everyone fits into a category, and a sub-category of a sub-category. Abandon any thought of being an individual defined by personality and belief, with aspirations to breadth of understanding, willingness to experiment.

In the world of the market you are fixed by age, education, income and a few expressed tastes into one category and no other. You no longer inhabit a society in common with other individuals. The market is not interested in what binds us together. It wants to know only how small and particular is the group into which we can reliably be corralled. It has a vision of a world of niches, where each one is separated from, wholly indifferent to, perhaps even hostile to, the values, wishes and interests of those in other niches. It thrives by fragmentation, by differentiation, through exclusivity rather than inclusivity, through disintegration rather than integration. It is a kind of marketplace apartheid. The citizen has ceased to exist, to be replaced by the target group. The market is not interested in who you are or what you believe, only what you will buy.

Set against this, a good society should offer a concept of citizenship which relates to others, which sees people in the round, and which adds what they have in common to what they are entitled to have for themselves. The market works in the opposite direction, leading to a balkanisation of identity, the elevation of the consumer, the purchaser, the customer over the broader, more humane categories of citizen, individual, member of the public, member of the family, part of the audience. A good society cannot be based on a rainbow coalition of minority rights or tastes; the more it is founded on such particularities, the less it will be founded on an inclusive sense of rights and duties open to all.

The members of the student group who began musing over the big issues of life fifty years ago have many of the ingredients of a good society. They meet because they like one another, because they value ideas, continuity, human exchange, and they do not set a cost on the activity. Their personal transactions are those of friendship. Where is friendship today? Not in the marketplace. Not in cyberspace. But then fraternity has always been the weak link in the holy Republican triumvirate.

A good society does not confuse ecstasy with enlightenment; it does not confuse atomisation with individuality; price and cost with value; exploitation with enterprise; reward with greed; cornucopia with choice; abundance with riches; elitism with exclusiveness; organisation with effectiveness; structures with relationships; noise with meaning.

The Mexican philosopher Ivan Illich was right to emphasise the importance of conviviality as a crucial social value. Unless some social activity, some urban project, some new institution contributed to an increase in human conviviality, then it was useless. As a single criterion for testing whether a policy or a decision advances the arrival of the good society, it cannot be bettered.

6 Populism Versus Elitism – Real Enemies or Bogus Opponents?

It is time to talk dirty, and where better to start than by using that politically dreaded 'A' word – 'art'. In the current pecking order of the politically incorrect, using the 'A' word is little better than the 'C' word – 'culture'. Soon after his arrival in the House of Lords, the architect and Labour peer, Richard Rogers, observed: 'Every time I mention the bogey word "culture" to British politicians, they just switch off.' Most of them are still doing so. Or if they do engage with the idea of culture, they try to avoid the issues by dismissing anything too difficult as elitist.

The problem is not that New Labour does not support the arts. Nor is it that New Labour hasn't significantly increased funding for them. The difficulty arises from the fact that they are frightened of uttering the word too publicly or too enthusiastically because their all-powerful focus groups do not like the sound of it. So even if New Labour is doing good to the arts by stealth, it does not want the electors to catch them in the act, or to be seen to be making life too easy for the arts. New Labour's search for popularity with everyone drives them to be populist about the arts. To be openly serious about the arts would be to look elitist, which is almost as bad as being Conservative. The arts – like skiing – are just not Islington and New Labour.

Now there are two more dirty words – 'populism' and 'elitism'. Are they useful intellectual scalpels for dissecting the condition and the practice of the arts? Or are they merely mindless boo words, useful to hurl abuse across a socio-political, intellectual divide, rituals in the dying exchanges in Britian's once traditional class wars? Peer down at the lower basement levels of debate and journalism where they are all too regularly employed.

In November 1999, the rebuilt Royal Opera House complex was opened. Most of the journalism covering this event – with one or two exceptions, notably among the architectural critics – was simply lazy. A programmed computer could have spewed out the stale trawl through the obvious files, the same old catalogue of sackings, resignations and death by a thousand shots in a TV documentary. Most of the news reporters stepped off the newsroom's taxi rank from hard duty on the latest criminal trial, clutching the news cuttings of yesteryear to their professional security blanket, the clipboard. They need the clipboard because they cannot be expected to know anything. None brought with them any personal knowledge of the arts or the arts world. Inevitably, they made no attempt to address issues such as the new House's artistic policy, to acknowledge the limitations of what even the increased funding levels could deliver in renewed or expanded repertory, least of all what role it might play in national arts policy and provision.

Instead, this massive new arts investment, this landmark statement about the arts in Britain, was scrutinised against one criterion – access – closely followed by questions – which were never corollaries – about whether the new House would be 'less elitist'.

The limitations of such an autopilot approach to journalism should be obvious. You cannot run an arts institution by judging it against one criterion, whether it increases access or not. That may be one of several dozen indicators of an institution's health and effectiveness. It may not be – it is not – the most important. To place an undue emphasis on it will merely distort the fundamental activity.

The second observation is this. Challenging the Royal Opera about whether it has stopped being elitist is first cousin to questions of a similar kind about wife-beating. The only honest answer to the question 'Will the audience change radically as a result of the new building?' must be 'don't be silly'. Few had the courage to give it.

It is a silly question because audiences do not change at the drop of a hat, through the absence of a black tie, with the creation of a see-through foyer, or at the behest of a new policy, even if it comes from the government. Audiences change and grow over a generation or more, and they need a broad range of conditions for their germination, development, nurture and flowering. One glance over the last fifty years at the proliferation of opera companies great and small, the length and breadth of Britain, or the growth of concert performances of opera, shows how much the demand and the audience have grown. Anyone who implies that audiences for opera have somehow not changed, as opera, theatre-going and society have changed, is either ignorant or dishonest.

(I am not for a moment saying that 'elitists' do not exist, that elitism is not a disease. We all remember the Covent Garden corporate supporter who told the notorious BBC TV documentary *The House* that what his guests liked about the Royal Opera was that being there *was* elitist. They knew that most people could not be there, and felt superior as a result. Several City businessmen have asked me in a helpful way whether I can't make the Barbican more exclusive and therefore more attractive to their clients.)

If rebutting the charge of elitism is an irrelevant answer to the wrong question, what should have been the right questions to ask about the value to the nation and the people of the new Royal Opera House complex? The only test by which the Royal Opera and Royal Ballet will be judged is the absolute quality of what they do. Audience broadening, education, outreach, diversity and so on are folded into the overall package of policies that any institution must follow. But they must start with the activity itself, the quality of the opera or ballet presented. Otherwise, why bother to increase access for anybody?

Had Sir David Webster, the first General Director of the Royal Opera after the war, not determined to turn Covent Garden into an international opera house, one that set standards for all, one which ultimately created demand for opera throughout the country, we would not now have the national operatic scene, the singers, the conductors, designers and producers that we do. That was not primarily why Webster did it, but the concentration on quality opened the door to the expansion of demand, the growth of audiences and the broadening of the overall experience. By contrast, to highlight one policy indicator, elitism, and treat it as if it is the only one that needs scrutiny and whose elimination can deliver success, is plain daft.

Of course, this debate is initiated not by the arts themselves but by politicians. The arts owe it to themselves, and any likelihood of long-term success for any government arts policy, to separate the immediately, politically convenient from what is artistically true and necessary. It is a debate that goes back a long way, certainly to Matthew Arnold. In a lecture at the British Library in 1997, Arnold's biographer, Nicholas Murray, reflected on the great man's views on culture. In many senses we are still struggling with his concepts to this day. In *Culture and Anarchy* written in 1869, Arnold defined culture as having four principal characteristics.

First, it should not be elitist nor a status symbol. (Chris Smith could agree with that.)

Second, culture should be socially useful since it is motivated both by the love of pure knowledge and by the moral and social passion for doing good. I think the Treasury, with its insistence that investment in the arts should be seen to 'do' something useful in the community, could agree with that, if, and it is a big 'if', the Treasury could be brought to accept that the good and the useful and the excellent are not always quantifiable in the form of instant saving or quick financial profit.

Third, culture should be dynamic not static, or as Arnold put it, it involves 'not a having and a resting but a growing and a becoming'. Only those enemies of the arts who try to corral them into a conservative, backward-looking enclosure labelled 'heritage' are likely to disagree with that definition.

Finally, Arnold insisted that culture should be profoundly democratic and inclusive rather than the preserve of the few. Everyone could agree with that, provided we could agree on what constitutes culture first. The relentless fragmentation of the word has created the difficulties of definition and acceptance that we now face. When it has become a mere suffix to almost any noun you want to stick on the front – from youth culture to pop culture to drug culture – it can no longer be used usefully as an idea on its own. Culture? What kind do you want? In this terminology, 'high culture' is merely another subset of all the other cultures, no better than any of them despite its pretensions to be superior. In fact, because the very word 'high culture' is tarred with a minority, elitist brush, it is probably judged to be a good deal worse than the other 'populist' forms of culture, authenticated as they are held to be by the numbers who practise or support them.

In other respects, Arnold's views would command little support today. He declared that what he called 'great men of culture' had a passion and a role for 'carrying from one end of society to the other the best knowledge, the best ideas of the time'. Today, I guess that anyone vain enough to suggest such an Olympian and missionary role for themselves would be greeted with the deafening roar of 'no thanks' and 'who do you think you are?' On the other hand, was Arnold wholly wrong in dreaming of people whose dedication to culture, that demanded to be propagated and shared, was so determined and passionate?

But elsewhere, Arnold's thinking stubbornly continues to resonate. In mid-nineteenth-century Britain, experiencing the advent of commercialised mass culture, he predicted that 'plenty of people will try to give the masses, as they call them, an intellectual food prepared and adapted in the way they think proper for the actual condition of the masses'. A century later, such transactions are dressed up in the plausible-sounding vocabulary of mass entertainment and marketing. But are they really any different from what Arnold warned against and clearly spotted as being both patronising and opportunistic?

Now, as then, those purveying mass culture do so in the name of choice and democracy, while in reality indulging in increasingly sophisticated forms of manipulation and reduction of choice. The very use of the words populism and elitism not only patronises the majority, it suggests that most people do not want or should not have the best available. It is the artistic equivalent of the view held in the 1940s that if the poor were given decent

council flats, they would use the baths to store the coal. I prefer
Nye Bevan, Labour's post-war Health Minister and his insistence: 'If it is good, it is good enough for the people.' It is no
coincidence that the very first British Arts Minister was his wife,
Jennie Lee.

What happens to these arguments if we take events at the
Barbican as an example: the polar opposites of populism versus
elitism emerge as a poor guide for judging either what we do, or
for establishing the principles that we adopt in our artistic
programming.

In November 1999, the Centre ran a series of five concerts
where leading international artists collaborated with artists
working in other media to create events of a different kind. For
obvious reasons, we called it 'Only Connect'. One night, the
Senegalese singer, Youssou N'Dour and his Super Etoile band
collaborated with the National Ballet of Senegal. The Barbican
was packed, the atmosphere so steamy some said they felt
themselves back in a tropical night in Dakar, an unlikely
thought. Diverse, undoubtedly. Accessible, surely. Excellent,
without a doubt. Was the event populist or elitist? The question
was totally irrelevant.

The same series found Michael Nyman and his band collabo-
rating with the video maker Chris Kondek in a disturbing work
about the way in which the victims of purges in Stalinist Russia
had their photographic images, public or private, airbrushed out
or defaced or destroyed. For some, Nyman sits squarely on the
populist wing of classical music; yet the subject matter was
remote and historical, though undoubtedly painful, and hardly
involved easy populist gestures. So where should such an event
have been pigeon-holed? How can such projects be restricted to
an existence in the sterile camps of either elitism or populism?
Come to that, why should we restrict them? Speaking for
ourselves at the Barbican, we won't play that game and we do not
need to.

When the Barbican presented all the works of Samuel Beckett
during three weeks in September 1999 in productions by the
Gate Theatre, Dublin, the season included *Breath*, the play that

runs for just thirty-five seconds. Beckett, with his people in dustbins, and plays where nothing happens – all remarks in inverted commas – is hardly populist. He just happens to be universal. The season was popular, since almost every production sold out. The audience was wonderfully varied in age, in their knowledge of the plays and in their nationality. Who would dare to dismiss as elitist a dramatist whose ideas, words, characters and philosophy have permeated the national vocabulary and the consciousness of the world?

There is a further question in this line of thinking. When the Barbican Gallery mounted its exhibition about the art of *Star Wars*, was that populist? If it was, how should the earlier exhibition at the Serpentine Gallery – that unimpeachable home of the ideologically cutting edge – of the work of the film designer Ken Adam have been judged? The arts world is far too various, diverse and flexible in its programming to make judgements based on elitism or populism anything but crude. The use of these words all too often reflects their origins in the broken shards of outmoded Marxism; that they have any life at all today springs from their convenience to the new prescriptions and shibboleths of marketing.

What is extraordinary and depressing is that these issues go back throughout the world of arts that Britain has known for fifty years since the creation of the Arts Council just after the Second World War.

In 1964, Benjamin Britten received the Aspen Award for Service to the Humanities. In his acceptance speech, he reflected on the artist's responsibility to his public. From Beethoven's Choral Symphony to Shostakovich's Leningrad Symphony, not forgetting the utterly different ways in which composers as various as Johann Strauss and Gershwin wrote for their respective publics, composers, he argued, have written for their people, for a community. 'I can find nothing wrong', said Britten, 'with the objectives of these men; nothing wrong with offering to my fellow men music which may inspire them or comfort them. Which may touch them or entertain them, even educate them – directly and with intention. On the contrary, it is the composer's duty, as a member of society, to speak to and for his fellow human beings.'

How successful Britten continues to be in speaking to his fellow men is magnificently confirmed by the productions in autumn 1999 of *Peter Grimes* at the English National Opera and that of *Billy Budd*, given by the London Symphony Orchestra at the Barbican. Indeed, the critic George Steiner said recently that in his view *Peter Grimes* was one of the few incontestable works of tragedy of the century.

But, Britten asked himself back in 1964, how far should an artist go in meeting people's demands? (He did not use the word populist but it is there hanging in the background.) Only the artist, he concluded, could test that against his conscience. He observed: 'There are many dangers which hedge round the unfortunate composer: pressure groups which demand true proletarian music; snobs who demand the latest avant-garde tricks; critics who are already trying to document for tomorrow, to be the first to find the correct pigeon-hole definition – these people are dangerous.' And we know that they are still at it today, though as they package artists into brands such as 'Britart' or 'YBS's, these activities are further from academic criticism or journalism, far closer to commercialism and marketing.

Britten observed that the artist, in turn, had a right to make demands of society, namely that 'his art shall be accepted as an essential part of human society and human expression, and that he shall be accepted as a genuine practitioner of that art and consequently of value to the community'.

And he wanted some engagement from audiences too. 'Music demands more from a listener than simply the possession of a tape-machine or a transistor radio. It demands some preparation, some effort, a journey to a special place, saving up for a ticket, some homework on the programme perhaps, some clarification of the ears and sharpening of the instincts. It demands as much effort on the listeners' part as the other two corners of the triangle, this holy triangle of composer, performer and listener.'

Now, I have a feeling that today's commissars who patrol the frontiers of 'access' and 'exclusion' will see such demands as too onerous by far. How dare an artist demand that the listeners make a prior effort to understand what they are about to hear? Is that not to exclude much of the audience in advance of a note being played? Yet the charge of exclusion, still less elitism, can hardly be laid at the doors of a composer who writes so powerfully about the most fundamental human emotions as Britten does, and continues to draw audience reactions of the greatest intensity. His works relate to human experiences of a universal kind, and transform them into an unforgettable and deeper form. That experience is open to all. Suggesting that the fullest understanding of such expression will come to those who make the greatest effort is not to exclude anyone.

Twenty years after Britten's observation, an outgoing Secretary General of the Arts Council, Roy Shaw, rounded off a collection of essays by addressing full-frontally the subject 'Art for the People'. Shaw was Secretary General from 1975 to 1983. As the son of a Sheffield steelworker, a tutor for the Workers' Educational Association, he had a particularly keen sense both of the arts and of the people. He believed that they had to be linked.

Shaw reminded readers of the obligation enshrined in the Arts Council's charter to 'develop and improve the knowledge, understanding and practice of the arts'. For him, education about the arts was the essential precondition for expanding understanding of them, a connection shrugged off or actually evaded by too many today. In fact, Shaw had to fight a running battle with colleagues who insisted that education was for schools and not the Arts Council. But, like Britten, Shaw recognised that without prior knowledge, access to the arts would always be an uphill task.

Fifteen years on, I think we have lost a lot of ground in this debate. Today the boot is on the other foot. It is arts organisations which are handed the main responsibility for access – in the intellectual rather than the physical sense. For they face the implied charge that it is the nature of the arts that they present – by definition, intrinsically difficult, and therefore excluding and elitist – which creates problems of access, that is to say, of understanding. If only the arts changed the nature of what they did, so the populist argument goes, access would be broadened quite easily. Such seems to be the language and assumptions behind much current Arts Council rhetoric. It is a total reversal of the going assumptions in Roy Shaw's time.

Behind it all is the stampede away from shared understanding about what constitutes the acceptable body of the arts. Recently, Channel 4 conducted a poll on the greatest tunes of the millennium. Just as we can wonder that Cliff Richard is the best known Christian figure in Britain, well ahead of the Archbishop of Canterbury – but then Cliff does actually talk about Christianity – so we should not be surprised that the poll found an overwhelming preponderance of votes for recent pop music. As that excellently irreverent Radio 4 programme, *The Now Show* commented, 'Isn't it extraordinary that all the best tunes in the millennium have been written in the last thirty-two years?' Eat your heart out, Hildegard of Bingen; stamp your foot, Henry VIII, over the disregard of 'Greensleeves'; cut your throat, Wolfgang Amadeus Mozart, over the rejection of *Eine Kleine Nachtmusik*; despair, Schubert, over the neglect of your *Trout*; groan, Beethoven, at such indifference to your Euro anthem. All, all take second place to Robbie Williams, etc., etc. If that isn't a populist verdict, what is?

But isn't it just a bit of millennial froth and fun? I do not think so. Any society that turns its back on its past, the accumulation of knowledge, experience, expression and understanding that has grown up over two millennia or more, is being extraordinarily reckless and overconfident about its ability to find all answers to all problems out of the understanding, the knowledge and the techniques that exist today. It is a huge gamble and a pointless one. But it is a gamble that the populist/elitist argument invites us to take.

What is curious is that this tension appears more acute now, when in many ways the position of the arts is notably stronger than it was just over a decade ago. In 1987, Roy Shaw worried about expanding the audience for the arts, about whether those without knowledge of the arts were being deprived of something desirable, or whether they were being patronised for lacking something they were entitled to reject.

In a lecture to the Lloyds TSB Forum in the summer of 1999, the Warden of Goldsmiths' College, Professor Ben Pimlott, did not see the problem at all. Addressing the subject 'Should the Arts Be Popular?', his somewhat jaunty and New Labour conclusion was that they are popular in ways that they never have been before. Pimlott cited as anecdotal evidence the universal availability of such high art images as Antony Gormley's *Angel of the North*, the presence of poems on the Underground, the universal currency of Damien Hirst's formaldehyde sheep. He might have thrown in Tracey Emin's notorious shortlisted Turner Prize bed, though whether as an example of living art demonstrating the capacity to speak eloquently about people's everyday concerns, or rather as a modish reflection of popular confessional culture, continues to be part of the broader debate.

In his rather Panglossian way, Pimlott sees the impact of the arts on society as remarkably pervasive: 'Even the aggressively philistine would have difficulty in missing completely the bombardment of arts programmes on radio, the classic remakes on television, the opera singers who introduce sports programmes, the arts hype news stories and the advertisements on London buses that play games with famous artistic images.'

I find it impossible to share such a cosy view. On radio, until Radio 4's *Today* programme treats the arts as regularly and in its own terms as it treats sport and money, I remain only partly reassured. Television schedules are full of planned 'zones' today. For the living arts, television appears to be a 'no-go zone'. Playing games with famous artistic images tells you nothing about our responses to the images in themselves. Munch's *Scream* may be recognisable but surely deserves better than reduction to a clichéd response of commercialised banality.

Wittingly or unwittingly, Pimlott may have revealed a change of attitude. New Labour's rhetoric about inclusiveness, about ending exclusion, eliminating elitism and so on, carries the assumption that the arts are an activity, a commodity perhaps, that should be available for mass consumption. In this respect, it might appear to represent an advance on Roy Shaw's time, when there were Marxist critics aplenty who saw art as something the bourgeoisie created, valued and consumed but wanted others to pay for. That was all very well for the bourgeoisie but it had nothing to do with the workers. Today's talk of the need for access, education, outreach and inclusion assumes that the arts should be available to everyone. Yet is such openness really an advance on previous attitudes?

Not long ago, the Culture Secretary, Chris Smith, said that at present only half the population had a connection to the arts of one kind or another; he wanted to see that extended to everyone. Some may be staggered to think that half the population does 'experience the arts' – whatever that means – but equally could be worried that the target of 'experience by everyone' sounds less like a laudable goal and more like a deliberately unattainable performance indicator.

To say there is a broader belief than before that arts are, or should be, for the people, does not solve very much. The drive for greater access and more inclusion does not imply that access should be to the arts as they are, or inclusion to the arts as at present constituted. The Trojan Horse in the argument is the implicit assumption that access to new audiences is denied by the arts because of what they are intrinsically; wider inclusion is prevented by the innate character of the artistic activities. In other words, it is up to the arts to change to allow greater access for those that find them difficult.

There would be little sympathy from today's advocates of great access to Britten's comments, that it is up to audiences to make an effort if they want to experience art fully. There would be none at all for Pierre Boulez's robust comment that art is difficult and that to complain about it is as pointless as complaining that a mountain you want to climb is rather high. Such views are decidedly not in the spirit of the times.

In this sense, we are back in Roy Shaw territory, with the arts insisting that they will never be widely understood without education, and the government saying that it is the job of the arts to transform themselves or at least to use their money to educate the missing audience.

Here the argument between elitism and populism fully engages. Elitism is held to represent the attitude that the arts – even in an arts world changing as much as I have indicated it is changing – will evolve in their own terms and according to their own imperatives. These include a recognition that education, outreach and access are practices which enrich any institution that adopts them enthusiastically. Populism demands that the only way the people will be engaged in any numbers is if the arts change their nature.

Behind it lies what I call in a deliberately ugly neologism, the 'marketisation' of values. Are the imperatives of the marketplace driving the judgement of values into wholly unacceptable – because quantifiable – directions?

Let me retrace my steps to Benjamin Britten when he asked himself, 'Where does one stop in answering people's demands?' At the point, he replied, where external demands 'make the composer self-conscious and he may be frightened into writing pretentious nonsense or deliberate obscurity. He may find himself writing more and more for machines, in conditions dictated by machines and not by humanity, or he may end up by creating grandiose claptrap when his real talent is for dance tunes or children's piano pieces.'

The pressures today, not just on composers but also on artists, come from the mechanisms of the market and of market research. Ask the market what it wants before you provide it. The dangers of doing this for any activity driven by values rather than quantities should be obvious. In 1999, the British Council conducted research about external images of Britain. On seeing the results, they were alarmed that Britain's internal self-image of innovation, self-confidence, irreverence and style had not registered itself deeply on target audiences overseas. The British Council concluded that those asked to represent Britain abroad at the Council's invitation, often authors and artists, were simply not projecting the right image. Instead, the Council would use footballers as representatives of real Britain today, and the strengths of, say, British architecture would be demonstrated by exhibitions of English Premier Division football stadiums.

It cannot have escaped the Arts Council's marketing department that most of the best footballers in the Premier League are overseas players. More brutally, they must have noticed that English international football was a second-rate export and that was even before England was formally relegated to the second division of world football.

By contrast, British artists, architects, composers, performers operate in the world first league of talent, demonstrating achievement in an incontestable and recognised way. Why are they not lauded more? Why did New Labour not speak up with pride for the architecture of the twelve stations on the Jubilee Line Extension rather than only emphasising the awfulness of the cost overrun of the project as a whole?

The answer is that football and footballers are held to relate to a mass audience; artists, architects and their like are held to relate to the minority. Footballers take part in activities that are seen as popular. Footballers are lifestyle heroes. Any company director taking home £50 thousand a week would be pilloried as a fat-cat exploiter. Roy Keane, the Manchester United captain, is applauded as worthy of his hire.

There has to be a consistency between what a nation does and how it is represented. To project Britain through representatives of an activity at which the country is second-rate and to turn your back on those where it is excellent is the sort of perversity that can only come from relying on the market rather than on common sense and values.

The BBC displays exactly the same symptoms. It achieved its greatness as an organisation driven by a strong set of shared values and a hugely strong common culture; these existed in a somewhat unsystematic, but not inappropriate, structure. The result was a broadcasting institution where programmes and audiences came first. Under the Birt regime, it was turned into an organisation where allegedly more efficient structures were imposed without reference to the values and purposes of the institution. The values and beliefs which had created and nurtured the broadcaster were replaced by systems and research which supported nothing and nourished no one. The very talk of values was pushed to one side because the BBC was saddled with a leadership incapable of articulating ideas which could not be quantified.

Yet among BBC staff, those actually making the programmes, public service values continue to exist, albeit in an underground manner. Where a leadership believes in systems and the staff believe in values, where the systems conflict with the values and make them hard to realise, you get the present state of the BBC, an institution which is on the verge of losing belief in doing what it was set up to do.

The BBC's leaders put the market before values. When this occurs in the world of the arts, the result is the massification of culture – where justification by numbers replaces justification by excellence or quality. When values are dictated by the market, the only values that count, the only activities that matter are those where the results or the effects can be counted or measured. Hence today's obsession with measurable performance indicators. This is why activities which enjoy the support of large numbers of people attract political approval.

But just what is the value of numbers in themselves? A friend with considerable contacts in television asked the other day: 'Can you tell me why eight million are better than one million?' Bigger, of course. Different, perhaps. Better?

What of the activities that cannot be measured, whose impact cannot be immediately determined, whose value cannot be established by the criteria of the market? In one sense, these can be pigeon-holed as a minority. Usually, being identified as a minority represents grounds for attracting support and protection. But an arts minority, and most arts activities are minorities of one kind or another, is automatically branded as an elite and an indigent one at that. Elites are – because it has become that kind of word – a bad thing that must be disowned and discouraged.

The implicit claim is that the arts must prove they are not a minority activity by showing that they are easy to use, do not have 'keep out' boards outside and that they are useful to society. But we have been here before. Showing that the arts are useful has not helped them to secure funding. And there are some awful historical warnings to keep in mind.

In the autumn 1999 edition of *Critical Quarterly*, Andrew Brighton, Head of Public Events at the Tate Gallery, made a provocative comparison between socialist realism in the former USSR and what he called the 'Command Culture' aspect of New Labour's cultural policies. Brighton found intriguing parallels between New Labour's statements and those earlier Soviet principles, which linked art to the aspiration for a better humanity, to the progressive struggle of the proletariat, and insisted on its identification with the ruling party.

Using close textual comparisons between written documents from New Labour and from the Soviet Union in the 1930s, Brighton demonstrated that the rhetoric of the two was strikingly close. When Tony Blair said in 1997 that the central role of the arts was 'the task of recreating the sense of community, identity and civic pride that should define the country', he was remarkably close to Lenin writing 'On Literature and Art'. When Chris Smith wrote that art and social good should converge and serve the people and social progress, according to Brighton, such views were a commonplace of Soviet cultural commentary.

When it came to condemnation of the elite, Brighton showed how the attack on the elite has long been a sustained theme of 'Labour speak' about culture. As Chris Smith wrote: 'The arts are for everyone. Things of quality must be available to the many, not just the few. Cultural activity is not some elitist exercise that takes place in reverential temples aimed at the predilections of the cognoscenti.' Brighton linked the language of an early 1990s Arts Council document, 'Towards a National Arts and Media Strategy', with current New Labour policies; these dismissed judgements about the arts made by 'creators, producers and critics' as 'essentially subjective'. The strategy paper demanded that the arts must be powerful agents for bringing together communities defined by 'geography, ethnicity, gender, religion or shared interests' and concluded that if the arts gave voice to what was previously silent 'they may be considered to be of high quality'.

Finally, Andrew Brighton linked the present government's determination to set criteria for access to the arts and through the medium of the new agency, Quest, to 'set targets, chase progress and take direct action to make sure our objectives are achieved'. The sheer *dirigisme* of this alignment of party demands with artistic roles carries too many echoes of Soviet cultural policy to be comfortable.

True or not, if these policies were implemented in practice, as Brighton implied that they would be, then the swing towards art that serves the people, society, the party, the government is stronger than we thought. Such populism is made easier to justify by the rolling-up of the alternatives in a pejorative way as being remote from the people, useless for the people and therefore irredeemably elitist.

Perceptive as his article was, Brighton did not notice that the old Marxist language of exploiters and exploited fitted snugly with current New Labour rhetoric about the excluded. The clear implication is that the excluded are actively kept out from the arts by someone – clearly the elite – who are not only damned for being what they are but for being elite excluders too. It is only a step from the idea of carrying responsibility for exclusion to the notion of being exploiters too.

Such exchanges reveal the polarised and confrontational vocabulary of populism and elitism as unsuitable for producing creative arts policies and helping understanding of and use of the arts to grow. The arts are useful, though they do not need to be, but they are useful in ways that cannot be determined at the time they are made. To insist on a socially, politcally, economically useful role that can be measured in its impact, wholly misses the point about the sheerly unexpected nature of the contribution that the arts can make to life and society.

They matter because they are unpredictable, unforceable, undirectable, and are not susceptible to plans, strategies and prescriptions. They yield their greatest benefits over years and often after initial scorn and rejection.

Part Two: Politics

7 I'm Worried About Tony*

Some readers will remember the familiar complaint of the eponymous writer of *Mrs Dale's Diary*, mother of all radio soaps. 'I'm worried about Jim,' she would confide anxiously, Jim being her doctor husband. Well, I am worried about the Prime Minister and the curious ideas he seems to have about the arts world; not just his ideas, but some significant blank spots in his view of them. Both – ideas and blank spots – account for the government's failure to treat the arts properly or sensibly. I am not the only one who is 'worried about Tony'. The Culture Department is worried sick too.

Let's start with those parties at Number 10. By all means invite the 'celebrity' world, the rock and pop world, the showbiz world, to bask in New Labour sunshine once. (Though judging by Damon Albarn's dismissal of the parties as 'disgusting and vulgar', perhaps a comment on Noel Gallagher, not all were impressed.) But to do so three times and to overlook the world of arts so thoroughly is pretty alarming.

Does Tony Blair really enjoy talking to Noel Gallagher more than he might, say, to John Tomlinson, the greatest Wagnerian bass in the world? Does he really enjoy chatting to Chris Evans or to Zoë Ball more than he might to, say, Beryl Bainbridge, Ian McEwan or Martin Amis? He could have invited fewer pop-group representatives and added a classical group such as the Lindsays, one of Britain's finest string quartets, or discovered the sprightly diversity of the Nash Ensemble players. He could have asked Dame Judi Dench or Juliet Stevenson, as well as Liz Dawn

* This article appeared in *The Times* on 11 March 1998.

of *Coronation Street*. As it was, they were very lop-sided lists, doing no sort of credit to Britain's internationally acclaimed arts achievers.

So, I'm worried about the Prime Minister because he is signalling that Oasis is as important to Britain as opera; that chat shows are as important as novels; that television soap-operas are more valuable than live theatre; and that all sorts of other key ingredients of the arts matter not at all. If it had happened just once, then it would not have been worth mentioning, but three times – not to speak of the official heavyweight Cabinet turnout at the Britpop awards (did all those ministers really want to be there?) – is no accident, comrades.

But there is worse to come. It is quite clear that the Prime Minister simply does not understand why the arts world is in such an uproar at New Labour's funding failures in the arts field. He is puzzled and has asked the Culture Ministry – more in anger than in sorrow – what is going on?

The puzzlement is said to stem from his conversion to the idea of the 'Creative Industries'. For in New Labour ideology, only the 'Creative Industries' count and the Government has been assiduous in devising policies directed to helping them. Given that, everything should be rosy. But the Prime Minister fails to understand that the 'Creative Industries' – film, video, TV, design, rock and pop – essential and admirable as they are, are only a part of the world of the arts, in some cases an applied extension of them. Having bought the idea of their importance and of the need to support them, he stopped looking beyond their boundaries.

In backing 'the arts that pay', and overlooking and undervaluing 'the arts that cost', Mr Blair shows himself to be the true son of Margaret Thatcher. In New Labour's Victorian world where the virtuous work and earn, the arts may (claim to) work but they manifestly do not earn – they are a cost to the community, a charge to the taxpayer, a burden on the citizen. This makes them less desirable – to New Labour – and certainly less deserving, than the virtuous worlds of the 'Creative Industries'. So their indigent representatives do not cross the portals of Downing Street.

But the confusion about where the arts start – or finish – and the creative industries begin goes deeper still. 'New Labour' was a triumphant exercise in re-branding – new people, new title, new logo, new colour, new clothes, new language – and now 'New Britain' has to be re-branded too. Out goes anything to do with the past, out goes anything to do with culture or continuity because it has been branded as – the killer word – 'heritage', and somebody has persuaded Mr Blair – or perhaps he needed no persuading – that the arts are just dead heritage; backward-looking, stuffy, uncreative and unsellable to foreigners.

Leave aside the fact that a casual glance at the arts scene in Britain – whether theatre, literature, dance, music or painting – will show them to be exploratory and innovative as well as aware of their historical roots, the h-word – a Reaganite formulation in any case, destructively adopted by the Thatcherites – has been foisted onto the arts and now hangs around their collective neck like the proverbial albatross. But it has been pinned on the arts by outsiders and is no part of the way the arts see or describe themselves. As a result of the pejorative use of the h-word, the arts are not only not included in the grand project of the re-branding or projecting of New Britain, they must be seen to be excluded in a very public way.

And one further bogey word has now been pinned onto the arts – 'elite'. I'm worried that Mr Blair is terrified of being caught even looking elitist. I know that Prime Ministerial Diaries are very full, but he does get to the theatre from time to time – he was at the Barbican only last week. Surely he could see for himself how ludicrously inaccurate is the smear of the alleged elitism or exclusivity of the arts audiences.

And this leads me to the core of my 'worries about Tony'. Simply, that the arts do not matter to him personally because they are a marginal and thinly-rooted side of his own experiences. He is a true child of the sixties; the rock and pop world is the one that he likes instinctively; he is simply not at ease in the arts world. His evident lack of esteem for it – as evidenced by the way his government treats it – springs from that essential personal discomfort.

Now, I may be wrong. I hope I am. But all his actions signal the reverse: that he has pop stars to his parties because he feels most comfortable with them. By contrast, the arts are now lumbered in the Prime Minister's mind with a heap of pejorative associations. We can expect little sympathy, minimal understanding, and feeble support for the financial crisis in which the performing arts now find themselves. Against this damaging, personal, Prime Ministerial mindset, weak protestations from the Culture Ministry count for nothing. That's why 'I'm worried about Tony'.

8 What Happened at Downing Street

A short time after I had voiced my 'worries about Tony' in *The Times*, the Prime Minister came to the Barbican to open a business conference on the need to take the Millennium Bug seriously. As is usual on these occasions, I was asked to meet and greet him. It was too good a chance to miss for pinning his ear back on the subject of the arts. It was 30 March 1998.

Neither he nor his staff – who were out in full force – made any reference to the article, barbed or otherwise. But after his speech, and a photocall in our foyer with the Covent Garden Soup Company – chosen because they were regarded as exemplary in their planning to mitigate the effects of the Millennium Bug – I escorted Tony Blair out of the building.

'Prime Minister, I would very much like the opportunity to come and talk to you about the arts. I realise you are frantically busy but I would value half an hour of your time at some stage.'

'We're not getting the arts right?' he queried as we strode along to the back-stage lift. 'Is it just about money?'

'It is about money,' I replied, 'but not just money. It is about the government's attitude to the arts as well. There is a perception problem.'

He replied politely that it would, of course, be helpful to have a chat some time. We left it at that.

On 14 April, I decided to take things further and wrote to the Prime Minister to see if I could prod him towards a meeting, supposing that he was inclined to be prodded. Within a fortnight, I got back a letter saying that he was going to hold a seminar on the arts at Number 10 and that the staff would contact me with details in due course. That due course came towards the end of May, with an invitation for 29 June 'to get across some of your ideas, hopes and fears about how Government policy should develop'. Soon after, invited participants to the seminar were asked to have individual, informal meetings with two Downing Street staffers – one a civil servant, the other a political adviser – about preparing the agenda in the light of the issues we thought important to raise.

Over the next few weeks, the preparatory staff work put into the seminar was detailed and impressive. Each participant was seen by the civil servants and each contribution was condensed into a series of agreed subject headings that covered the topics that seemed common to most.

In the meantime, I took the opportunity to consult some of my closest artistic colleagues and partners, such as the London Symphony Orchestra and the Royal Shakespeare Company, to make sure that I was representing their views accurately and as fully as possible. Their comments boiled down to four areas of concern. First, money. All of them said the resources lost as a result of four years' cash standstill without an uplift for inflation had to be restored. This loss was, after all, the main cause of the arts funding problem. (Later, Richard Eyre in his Report confirmed that there was an exact match between the accumulated deficits of most organisations and the impact of the standstill funding. The deficits did not reflect bad management so much as sustained underfunding.) If after having their core funding restored these arts bodies received an annual uplift for inflation – meaning they received no more, but no less in real terms – and a three-year settlement on this basis, then they could survive. It would not be riches. It would not be more money in real terms, but it would mean an end to cuts.

Second, my colleagues expressed deep concern about the subject I had raised in my *Times* article: the apparent dichotomy in the government's mind between the so-called 'creative industries' and the arts. 'In reality,' said one friend, 'they are one. But the government has put a knife between them.'

Third, there was the deepest anguish about the Lottery. Of

course, it had put millions into capital funding that would not have been available otherwise – to put it in industrial terms, this was money for plant, not for productions or wages. But in the mind of the public, 'the arts are getting millions from the Lottery and they are still moaning.' Collectively, ministers and arts leaders had made a miserable job of telling the public what Lottery money was for and what it was not for. The impression given – and not contradicted – was that the arts world had arbitrarily grabbed a large sum of the 'People's Lottery cash' and was complaining that it was not greater than it was. The fact that it was Parliament which had decided the apportionment of the Lottery money was ineffectually stated and inadequately emphasised.

When, too, the Arts Council had tried to divert some Lottery cash into actual arts activity by devising the 'Arts for Everyone' programme (one heavily inclined to educational schemes that broadened the base of those who could enjoy the arts), the experience of A4E, as it was called, had turned into a ruinous bureaucratic nightmare. The volume and value of applications wildly outstripped the sums of money dedicated to A4E; the Council's officers were drowned in the flood. When the overwhelming majority of applicants were rejected, the bitterness felt at the hours of scarce time, energy, human and other resources wasted in submitting proposals doomed not to be taken seriously was huge. In this context, anger about diversion of money from the arts to the management consultants who either drew up the schemes or evaluated them – using up some twelve to fifteen per cent of the total value of grants given, according to one of my colleagues – was profound and strongly held.

To these common complaints, I identified a further anxiety: even when money was granted, so many strings, forms and conditions were attached that it was far less useful than a single increase in unrestricted funding would be. The danger was that a single grant to an arts institution would now only be supplemented by a series of discrete additional grants – for, say, education, access, outreach – each of which would be subject to individual scrutiny as to its effectiveness in delivering the performance targets devised for it. Apart from increasing the amount of bureaucratic supervision involved, such a process denied any particular arts institution the opportunity to spend the total grant as it thought appropriate, bearing in mind the agreed overall aims of that institution.

Finally, as I talked more widely with friends throughout the arts, there was the matter of the Dome. 'The arts are short of money,' said one friend, 'but the Dome never is. It is a monster. The government has lost credibility with it.' Yet almost everyone felt that even to raise the matter at Downing Street would be counter-productive in view of the government's total commitment to it as a flagship project of its first term in office. Still the sense of outrage about the money spent on the Dome is almost impossible to overstate. Not long ago, I asked one of Britain's greatest pianists what he would say to Tony Blair if he met him. 'First, I would say that I voted for you and I did so because I thought that Britain badly needed a change of direction. Second, that I am now very disillusioned by the way the arts have been treated and by the lack of importance the government gives to them. Then, I would tell him that at a time when the arts are struggling to make ends meet, the sums of money spent on the Dome are just shocking.'

A few days before the seminar, Dennis Stevenson, the outgoing Chairman of the Tate Gallery, who had been named as the chairman of the assembled group of twenty arts worthies, rang us all up, checked that we would have the opportunity to say what we wanted within the agreed format, and invited us to add anything as the discussion took place. He had divided the seminar into five areas for discussion, to give it a focus without stifling debate. The main topics identified in the pre-seminar briefings were listed as: financing the arts; reform, change and management; education; access; and institutions and their inter-relationships.

Dennis's final message was this: 'Don't go on too much; keep to two minutes or less for your first statement. And a bottle of champagne for anyone who keeps a subsequent intervention to less than a minute.' (I do not know who, if anyone, won it.)

For all that twenty leading arts figures were going to talk about a world publicly identified as being in a state of crisis, the media got no advance wind of it. This speaks volumes for the discretion of those involved, but then they were all serious players. They included Ruth McKenzie, Director of Scottish Opera, Trevor Phillips, Chairman of the London Arts Board, Sir Simon Rattle, Genista McIntosh, Managing Director of the Royal National Theatre, Neil McGregor, Director of the National Gallery, Neil Cossons of the Science Museum, Melvyn Bragg, and others of a similar standing. Given the participants, had news of the event broken over the preceding weekend, the advance speculation and inevitable position-taking would have made sensible discussion difficult if not impossible. You can imagine the tabloid headlines – 'Labour in Luvvie Love-In' and such like – that would have prejudged the tone of the debate and any decisions reached. As it was, the outward calm and lack of hype served to make the occasion and the atmosphere constructive.

We were called for 3 p.m. on 29 June on a warm summerish afternoon, that comparative rarity in the summer of 1998. After twenty minutes in the Downing Street antechamber with a cup of tea, Tony Blair, Chris Smith, Geoffrey Robinson (then Paymaster General at the Treasury), and the Downing Street staffers appeared. My hunch from the beginning was that the door was already open to the possibility of an increase in arts funding. Holding the seminar at all was clear recognition of a need to put things right or at least righter. Whatever outsiders might think of the arts leaders assembled, to have called them in to Downing Street, listened and then to have given the arts nothing would have been a more obviously calculated rejection of the arts as a whole than all those Number 10 drinks for rock stars and pop presenters. Such a slap in the face was unlikely but, if my guess was wrong, mere tea and sympathy might be all we got. Whatever the underlying anxieties, the atmosphere in the Cabinet Room was relaxed, non-confrontational and open in every sense.

For a start, there was a refreshing readiness to concede fault on both sides: on the government's that there had been insufficient dialogue with the arts world; on our side, that arts funding administration had been 'something of a shambles', and that it had to be straightened out rather quickly. The ghost of the Royal Opera hung balefully over the proceedings but, like the Dome, it was a subject put to one side as something that would muddy the overall argument not clarify it.

I was struck, too, how ready the arts side was to admit past weakness in giving grants. There was a whiff of Admiral Byng in the air. If arts funding bodies were to recover public credibility as rigorous dispensers of public money, then some recipients would have to be taken out and shot, '*pour encourager les autres*'. The Greenwich Theatre would not be the last institution to receive this treatment. If factories closed, then why not theatres or orchestras? The arts world must take decisions, said one leading administrator, justify those decisions and then stick to them. Too often, said another, a hard decision to cut support for an institution was taken but was then undone because of 'blind-side' lobbying. If the arts were to be seen to run themselves seriously, such openness to lobbying had to be stopped.

As the ninety-minute meeting wore on, it seemed to me that what we were doing was to put on the table, unconsciously at first, the elements of a new compact. The representatives of the arts were present not merely as penitents or supplicants. They were there – in diplomatic-speak – as *demandeurs* too. What were we demanding?

I took the opportunity to make the case that the root of the problem was the government's perceived misrepresentation of the priority it attached to the 'creative industries' over the arts. I had prepared a short statement of less than two minutes on the subject as agreed with Dennis Stevenson who cued me in at the appropriate time:

'There is a real perception deficit about the government's approach to the arts. Over the last decade, the extent to which the arts play an important part in economic regeneration, job creation and tourism has become well understood, evaluated and costed. Phrases such as "cultural industries", "creative industries", evolved as a way of dragging arts subsidy funding in on the coat-tails of those commercial offshoots of the arts.

'In practice, the subsidised arts and the creative industries are part of a continuum of activities, skills and attitudes. They inter-relate, interact and feed into and off one another in a constructive, informal way. What has happened under this government is that – by design or inadvertence – a knife has been put between the subsidised arts and the creative industries. The latter have been held up as publicly and economically valuable, and an integral part of the re-branding Britain exercise; the former held up as less valuable, less relevant to New Labour's reformist project, more costly, and backward- rather than forward-looking.

'I know that this perception – or misperception – is widely felt by the arts world and by the public at large. I suggest that it does the government no good and the arts much harm that it is allowed to persist. I believe that it can be healed but it needs the government's own words and actions to show that it values the arts not because they need subsidy but because in the widest sense that subsidy is an investment in the nation's spirit.'

The debate broadened, after a marvellously idealistic state-ment from Richard Eyre, whose public status has become that of resident defender of values and seer of the non-material (but not immaterial). The arts world was looking for a recognition that the arts are not a commodity and cannot be treated as if they were part of the market in commercial arts. We wanted acknowledgement, too, that the arts have been under-funded for years and that the grant of subsidy does not by itself mean that the money is spent wastefully.

We asked at least for the arts to be treated on a par with sport – sports activity in schools is regarded as a key to the national health; but why is arts activity not seen in exactly the same light? 'Art is at the heart of the nation's health,' said one participant. Arts are essential to ease the nation's 'poverty of spirit'. Another stated roundly that the arts had been marginalised and under-funded for years by successive governments and it was time for this to stop.

In return, the arts side recognised that we needed to play our part in creating a new compact with the nation as well as with the government. 'There is a democratic deficit in the management of the arts,' said one of those present. Someone else urged arts institutions to be more confident in the skills they had within themselves and to offer those skills to the outside community.

But we did not just examine the philosophical basis of the position of arts in society. We discussed money, not in terms of volumes of pounds and pence alone but in terms of strategy. Lottery money must continue to be additional to the Treasury's contribution from national taxation revenues. The Lottery grant cannot be endlessly cannibalised to make up for the sustained shortcomings of the basic grant in aid.

I summed up what my artistic colleagues had told me they regarded as four essential elements in a financial 'Blair Settlement' for the arts. First, restore the value of the arts grant to what it was before the cash standstill four years ago. Second, give the arts a fixed annual grant which included an annual uplift for inflation. Third, give the arts a three-year settlement, allowing freedom to plan for more than one year at a time. Finally, tell us that from now on we are on our own. Anyone who could not manage on that basis would deserve whatever came to them.

I am breaking no confidence in saying that I and others thought that the Prime Minister used a very significant phrase in his summing up − it has already been reported in the press. 'We must write the arts into our core script,' he offered.

I gave two examples of other political leaders who had 'written the arts into their core scripts' and embodied them into their own core public acts. The former President of the Federal German Republic, Richard von Weizsäcker, would fly from Bonn to West Berlin to attend the opening of the Deutsche Oper's latest production of Wagner's *Ring* cycle. When Pierre Boulez was lured back to France to set up his musical research centre, IRCAM, in the Baubourg (the Pompidou Centre), he had been personally wooed by President Pompidou at a private dinner.

Will Tony Blair be as naturally inclined to interleave the arts into his core script in his own appropriate way?

Was the sense of mutual understanding at the seminar between the government and the arts real or had we been enmeshed in the web of the spinmasters? Remember what happened before the budget, said one wary participant. There was a leak that the Chancellor of the Exchequer, Gordon Brown, was going to find £40 million to 'save the museums'. On budget day, what they actually got was £6 million, but so tied up with conditions that, as one senior Whitehall hand observed with relish, 'it was a three card trick; now they saw it, now they didn't'.

So as we came out of Downing Street, we knew that the government had listened to the arts; but would they hear? Two weeks later we knew that they had done both. Gordon Brown's comprehensive survey of government public spending yielded £290 million extra for the arts over three years. When Chris Smith, the Culture Secretary, announced the details, the news that the newly-structured Arts Council would have £30 million, £40 million and £55 million extra in each of the next three years revealed a significant evolution in the government's attitude towards funding the arts.

What caused the change of mind and what part did the Downing Street Seminar play in it? Undoubtedly a primary reason for the transformation was that the arts world made a fuss. Whether it was another outburst from Sir Peter Hall or Sir John Drummond in his now-celebrated Royal Philharmonic Society lecture in January 1998, singly and collectively these very public questionings of the Blair Government's approach to the arts first ruffled Downing Street, then disturbed it, and finally drew ministers into action. There was a good measure of brutal political calculation involved. 'Look,' said a highly-placed Blair adviser to a musical friend, 'neither Brown nor his Treasury team are remotely interested in the arts and Tony isn't wildly interested himself. But they don't like the fuss, they see it will not go away and if a few million will buy it off, then it's worth paying.'

Against this background, the Arts Seminar had a specific function to fulfil. We had to convince Tony Blair that the arts world was a serious group of people; that we were professional about looking after money as well as delivering our particular art form. 'Prime Minister,' said Dennis Stevenson at one point in the meeting, 'everybody around this table runs an arts institution efficiently and effectively. That is one of the reasons that they are here.'

I suspect that the presence of the Paymaster General, Geoffrey Robinson, showed that sums of money for the arts had already been pencilled into the Comprehensive Spending Review. Whether figures at the higher end or the lower end of the range finally emerged in Gordon Brown's statement would be affected by how the arts world showed itself at the seminar.

I believe that the seminar worked, too, because of some shrewd handling by Chris Smith. While the Treasury and Downing Street can see – and see off – a 'give us more money' campaign at several leagues' distance, no one could trace Smith's fingerprints back to the general outcry from the arts. Yet there is no doubt that the Culture Ministry quietly fanned the voices of protest once it knew that Downing Street's anxieties had been aroused. These discreetly encouraged public protests both strengthened the case for the arts themselves and probably saved the ministerial skin of Chris Smith.

The Culture Secretary deserves credit at another level. For months, as the arts protests grew, Smith remonstrated that we should be patient and wait for the outcome of the Spending Review. No one paid much attention or believed in his capacity to deliver, but the final outcome proved him more right than many had believed possible.

One hopes that Tony Blair took away some serious messages from the seminar. First, that arts and museums make their own justification for subsidy. Subsidy is not a second best to the workings of the market but a vital factor in its own right, creating stability in institutions that foster innovation and high artistic standards. Second, that funding without an uplift for inflation for four years – cuts in everything but name – had predictably caused an acute financial crisis and Lottery money would not solve it. Third, that the arts world had to develop what Richard Eyre had identified as a 'new contract for the arts' between government, the people and the arts institutions.

But this Prime Minister always insists on something for something. In return for a large boost for arts funding, the Government is demanding action. Not just in the well-worn areas of excellence, access, education and economic development, but over actual reform. The arts must deliver better decisions, provide evidence of a clear strategy, ensure an end to bail-outs for the incompetent or terminally indecisive. Above all, the arts world must hope to be speedily delivered from the malignant shadow of the continuing mismanagement by the Royal Opera which Downing Street is not alone in seeing as having harmed every other arts institution.

The dialogue did not end at the doors of Downing Street. We were all invited, on that occasion and later by letter, to write to the Prime Minister with further observations on the state of the arts. After a good deal of thought over the summer, I decided to concentrate on an area that had not arisen at the seminar, that was not generally linked to the arts but which was central to the success of the arts: that is to say the roles of the broadcasters. They have a major responsibility to the arts. They were getting away scot free from scrutiny in this area. So, in September 1998, I wrote to Tony Blair turning his attention to this overlooked area of arts policy.

I am concentrating on a subject that did surface at the seminar – the relationship between education and the arts, to which you refer in your letter – but I want to add a further, so far missing, ingredient to the discussion which could even be its missing link. Fortunately, this falls squarely into the remit of Chris Smith's department – it is the role of broadcasting and the responsibility of the broadcasters in relation to the arts.

The damaging effect that cuts in music education have had in producing a generation deprived of basic access to music in the curriculum is well known. Simon Rattle and others have spoken to you eloquently about this. But the role of the broadcasters in enabling access and education about the arts to occur has been largely overlooked. It is curious that the broadcasters have stood aloof, in practice and in theory, in the very intense debate that the arts have been having with government in the last year or so. I think this is a grave, though perhaps not an accidental, omission on their part.

The fact is that in the area of television, there has been a massive retreat from arts coverage journalistically, and from arts programming over the last decade. While the BBC has always played the greatest role in the area of arts promotion, one would expect it to do so as an essential part of its public service remit. Indeed, in the past, it has shouldered this responsibility freely and enthusiastically. It is the BBC's retreat from the arts which is the most glaring, both in radio and television.

Put simply, if the broadcast media only broadcast news about the arts when there is a scandal, if they do not treat the arts as an essential part of society and social activity; if they have no language for addressing arts and their audiences and regard them as a vulnerable and undesirable part of the programme mix, then the audiences of the future are denied access to the arts because they will have received no education or information about them.

A review of the way in which all TV and radio arts coverage has declined drastically in recent years is simple to carry out and would be instructive and alarming. Without improved coverage from the broadcasters, the commitment to reintroduce music education into schools is seriously weakened. The arts community can only do so much in the area of access to and education about the arts. Without a positive and active role from the broadcasters, much of your strategy to put the arts at the core of your political concerns and public interests is weakened.

I urge you and Chris Smith to engage the broadcasting

authorities – privately or publicly – in discussion about their responsibility to the encouragement of the arts. In the case of the BBC, this discussion should centre on their proclaimed role and special responsibility as a public service broadcaster. But I do not think that the commercial broadcasters should be allowed to wriggle off the hook of arts provision on the grounds that they must maximise audiences, advertising and income.

I believe that the progressive retreat from a convinced commitment to arts broadcasting – of the arts and about the arts – is an important factor in the steady decline in audiences. The arts world cannot address access and education by itself – the broadcasters have a role and responsibility and it seems to me and others essential that they acknowledge it and take it up. From your government's point of view, a three-way partnership between government, the arts, the private sector would be vastly strengthened by the involvement of the broadcasters. We would move from an unstable triangle to a soundly based square. Honestly, I do not believe you – or we – can do it without the broadcasters.

There is, in short, still a long way to go before all the forces that can create a healthy, varied, dynamic arts world have been mobilised. There is a wholeness to the ecology of the arts world; the broadcasters are an integral part of it, but are too often treated as if they are mere observers. Trying to make artists and the arts institutions healthy by themselves only addresses, at best, two-thirds of the problem. Unless the broadcasters are part of the diagnosis and part of the solution, then the arts will always be struggling against much of the prevailing zeitgeist. Only government can make sure that the broadcasters play their parts in enhancing education about the arts, easing access and allowing familiarisation with what the arts have to offer. Without them, it will be an uphill struggle.

So Downing Street did start the dialogue between politicians and the arts. Only an optimist would claim that it was more than the end of the beginning.

9 When Being Creative is Not Enough*

It was rash of Chris Smith to put down his thoughts on the arts just when early hopes were fading that Labour might be the salvation of an arts community well and truly on the ropes. After all, the Tories had been notorious philistines. True, Margaret Thatcher had a Henry Moore maquette at Number 10; John and Norma Major were regular opera-goers (or rather Covent-Garden-goers, a somewhat different proposition). But by and large, the Tories – if they went to anything cultural – felt more at home with the smart and exclusive.

Not that Labour MPs were widely visible at plays or concerts, come to that, nor were MPs of any stripe or persuasion. There is a case for early closing in the Commons on one night a week with an obligation on MPs to attend something cultural, preferably in their own constituency. They would certainly understand the arts better and might be better politicians into the bargain. While such a dramatic shift of attitude and habit was too much to expect of New Labour, many would-be Labour courtiers in the arts during the Opposition wilderness years had convinced themselves that a new government would be both different from the Tories and better for the arts. They had to be, didn't they?

Well, the arts world – Labour, LibDem or Tory – soon discovered that just because Labour under Harold Wilson had created the first ever Arts Ministry where Jennie Lee gained an iconic reputation for what an arts minister should be, that was no guarantee that a new Labour government – or rather a 'NEW Labour' government (not quite the same thing) – would pick up

* Chris Smith's book *Creative Britain* was published in May 1998.

the reins where Jennie Lee had set them down. At this critical
moment of burgeoning disillusion in the arts world in the
summer of 1998, Chris Smith's book appeared. It was greeted
with howls of derision, bordering on hate, and not just from
leaders in the arts. All the frustrations, and more, felt by the
beleaguered art world spilled out into the reviews. What was the
book's crime? That it was not a paean of belief in the arts; it was
not a cultural manifesto or personal credo, nor a statement of
philosophy. It was a compendium of speeches, a *tour d'horizon*, a
workmanlike departmental summary, in effect, of his efforts to
date as Secretary of State for Culture, Media and Sport.

Much water has flowed under the bridge since that lurid
publication day in the summer of 1998, but neither the book nor
its philosophy has been disowned by the author or his
government. Since the operating principles and beliefs it
describes are still valid and must be assumed to drive government
policies to the arts, both deserve a more considered examination.
My own view is that the book is by no means as bad as the
reviewers suggested, but that good or bad, better or worse, it
cannot simply be rejected. If it describes the approach of the
government of the day and of the foreseeable future, the arts
world had better take it into account in framing its own
expectations and behaviour.

For a start, Chris Smith's heart is clearly in the right place. He
says a lot of the right things – I mean things that reflect an
interest in and respect for the arts as something necessarily
distinct from other activities and to be valued because they are
different. That is a good start.

He repudiates 'Cool Britannia' as a slogan for the government's approach to the arts. But he is extremely disingenuous in
blaming media reporting and wilful misinterpretation by outsiders for the misunderstanding surrounding that glib phrase and
the derision heaped on it. Government spokesmen enthusiastically adopted the term and assiduously deployed it so long as it
suited them. As soon as even the pop stars, who were at the heart
of the 'Cool Britannia' phenomenon, objected to the phrase and
their exploitation by it, the government backed off very fast.

Smith's public rejection of it is part of that process. Still, rejected it is.

He gives several reasons for defending state subsidy of the arts (yet oddly omits enabling the arts to continue to exist as one of them). He sets out specific ways in which culture and creativity make a vital contribution to a healthy society. He recognises the value of the English language to Britain – an asset that others will seize as their own instrument of international communication while we often undervalue it as our own national means of expression and the definer of our identity. He is not afraid of the idea or practice of preserving heritage – a ball and chain of a concept that right-wingers strapped onto the arts, and that left-wing populists found it convenient to kick pejoratively. He accepts the concept of 'heritage' as a simple acknowledgement that the achievements of the past, particularly its physical monuments, are worthy of respect and maintenance.

Smith has a nifty line in using uplifting quotations (hats off to the Department's reference library, no doubt), carefully rationed out on a speech-by-speech basis. I hope he has restored some of them to the general currency of public debate. Each one makes a contribution to the case for the necessity, the legitimacy, of the arts.

Thus, Hazlitt: 'The arts do not furnish us with food or raiment, it is true; but they please the eye, they haunt the imagination, they solace the heart. If after that you ask the question, *Cui bono?* there is no answer to be returned.' It may be difficult and unfashionable to make an absolute claim like that a hundred years after Hazlitt, but it remains one worth attempting.

George Bernard Shaw is invoked: 'The statesman should rank fine art with, if not above, religion, science, art education and fighting power as a political agency.' But fifty years after GBS's hortation, it remains just that: an ideal rather than a reality. Commitment to the 'fine arts' ranks lower in governmental concerns than it did when GBS wrote. And Smith includes some neat, contemporary quotes to show that the search for the conclusive argument in favour of the arts is a continuing mission. For example, it was the Gulbenkian Foundation that said: 'The

arts are the principal trainers of imagination.' Smith himself
carried over a personal observation when he changed portfolios
from Health to the Arts: 'Health is a *sine qua non*; but culture is a
raison d'être.' Yet, while these statements are raised like well-
meaning flags of principle to show where the author stands, his
ultimate failure to attach policies to such principles makes them
appear like mere flags of convenience rather than active calls to
the colours.

In another area of his departmental responsibility, Chris Smith
makes practical points about the new era of multi-channel TV
and the BBC's role in it. As a strong supporter of public service
broadcasting, he sees the BBC role as the benchmark of quality
programme making – a role which is more not less essential in an
'era of viewing choice'. He insists that viewers want to watch
good programmes rather than themed channels; channels are,
after all, a technological and marketing construct. Programmes
provide viewing in audience-friendly sizes and formats. More
recently, in an article in the *Radio Times* in September 1998,
Smith has written with even greater emphasis about the
importance of the BBC remaining a programme-driven organisation: 'If the BBC continues to produce high-quality programmes,
it will be difficult for other channels, who require an additional
payment, to offer something inferior and get away with it.' And
he added a significant warning: 'I've told [BBC] senior management that the judgement by government and public will be based
primarily on quality, not ratings.' Taking his book and these
subsequent statements together, the Blair Government's uncritical endorsement of the market-driven, multi-channel-directed
policies of Bland and Birt at the BBC looks very odd. On this
evidence, BBC bosses are significantly out of kilter with what
Smith himself believes about the primacy of programme excellence as the Corporation's main function. Equally, the BBC's
obsession with research-driven, ratings-directed programme making sits uneasily with such a clear direction from their political
master.

The BBC is not the only subject where the more you read
Creative Britain, the more the questions and doubts crowd in. For

instance: in the government's continuing insistence on the need for accessibility the arts are implicitly reproached for making themselves remote, exclusive and inaccessible. Yet this is to beat a horse that does not exist. One or two corporate subscribers to Covent Garden may have stated freely in the notorious television documentary *The House* that they wanted their clients to feel they were coming somewhere exclusive, but I know of no one in the arts, or in a serious audience, who wants to keep anybody else away from a performance. Rather the opposite: we clamour to get people in and are active in devising programmes and pricing strategies to help that to happen.

At the same time, however, certain things cannot be made more intellectually accessible than they are. Four-and-a-half hours of Wagner or Messiaen's *St Francis of Assisi* are just that; long, and difficult as well. Such masterpieces, and many others, are supremely worth the effort. If to be accessible involves making an artistic event easier than was its creator's intention, then the call for 'accessibility' is a call for the removal of most of the things that make a work into a work of art. I know Chris Smith neither believes that nor wants that to happen. Yet the facile chanting of the 'access' mantra slides away from facing up to its complex implications.

The real problem is less one of approachability than of an indifference to or actual rejection of the arts by wide sections of society. This reflects a generation of educational practice where the historic arts – to coin a phrase – have been undervalued because they have been labelled by some educational theorists and teachers as 'inaccessible', 'irrelevant' and a variety of other pejorative words. If the government truly cares about the arts, it must address the problem of 'rejection' quite as energetically as the one they now choose to emphasise: that of 'access'. The latter is the symptom; the former is the cause of the problem. Of course, the cure might be a different mantra – education, education, education – but that would depend on what is put into the educational curriculum.

But the fundamental weakness of the Smith philosophy is the all-inclusiveness of his definitions. It is all very well – or not very well – to set aside as too remote from everyday experience Matthew Arnold's definition of culture as embracing 'the best that has been known and said in the world'. But to slip into preferring Bobby Kennedy's shallow definition of culture as 'that which makes life worthwhile' – as Chris Smith does – is to believe that playing tag football around the pool at Camelot, or sleeping with Marilyn, is culture. Enjoyable of course; but culture? In any case, the Kennedy clan are unreliable witnesses to enlist in the support of the arts. After a performance on the White House lawn by the pipes and drums of the Black Watch, Jackie Kennedy confided in a staffer: 'The President really enjoyed himself. He did suffer so when Casals played here.'

So too the inherent dangers of these over-stretched definitions are exposed in the use of the key Smith word 'creative'. I can see why he wants to rescue the word from the constriction of being used to describe, say, only Shakespeare, Tolstoy, Michelangelo and Picasso and never anyone lower in the pantheon or anything other than the most original and intense acts of artistic creation. This is the Himalayan application of the word that leaves 99.9% of humanity stigmatised with the label of 'uncreative'.

But in this rescue attempt, Smith credits almost every activity with any element of individual thought with being 'creative'. Advertising? Of course. Videos and television, naturally. Antiques? Up to a point. Fashion? You bet. Computer games? Certainly. Would he include 'creative accounting' too? Of course there is a 'creative' element in all of these activities, but when all are wrapped up in the same word, it rapidly loses any real value. Is the creativeness applied in all these widely diverse activities really the same?

And sooner rather than later, Smith faces the tricky question. If these activities – useful, enjoyable, entertaining as they are – are creative, what are the arts? Are they more creative than the above, just as creative, or less creative? He does not say. Are they – harder still – different in their creativity from the 'creative industries'? He does not attempt an answer. For the great evasion in the Smith book is that he never addresses the question of the real distinctiveness of art. He hoped to dodge the question by making the word 'creative' all-embracing. But the wider the doors are opened, the more glaring is the scale of his evasion.

For the arts get left behind in the crush to get through the doors of inclusiveness, especially as earning money appears to be part of the price of the entry ticket. 'Creative industries' – as defined by Chris Smith – are sometimes original, often ingenious and frequently inventive. They are also lucrative, or if not then they go out of business. Some arts – or certainly some artists – get rich. But does failure to make money from your work disqualify you from being considered an artist? And if an artist does not make ends meet, does this necessarily invalidate his work? If an arts institution does not earn its keep, does it fail to qualify for the accolade of being part of the 'creative industries'? In these thickets Smith does not go hunting. He has no way through them. But the thickets are of his own planting.

The trouble is that he will not come clean. What is art? And does he value it even if it is not a creative industry? Recently, Chris Smith declined to differentiate between 'high and low art' because he said that would involve making a value judgement! Does he make no value judgements as a politician or as a private individual? What is the point of being Secretary of State for Culture if you will not risk making some value judgements? To highlight the importance of the creative industries, to celebrate British achievements in them, and to mark the extent to which they are a truly post-industrial part of the modern economy are all useful activities. But they are matters that sound more like the province of the Department of Trade and Industry.

And the more Chris Smith talks of these industries, the further we are from the arts. Do they matter because they are good for the soul? Are they useful as a kind of social purgative, like rhubarb? Do they have an intrinsic value that society needs to encourage if it is to stay more than a materialist creation? Do they matter at all? If so, how much are they worth, and do they repay the cost? Specifically, how much are they worth to New Labour? Answers are needed to such questions if Britain is to have an arts policy and a flourishing arts world which will last far,

far longer than 'Cool Britannia', 'Creative Britain' or 'Rebranding Britain' – which are merely modish diversions. If Chris Smith could answer the fundamental questions about art, he might find that the creative industries flourished even more as a result.

10 Thoughts on the Thoughts of Chairman Gerry*

Not long ago, a leading British arts institution was looking for a finance director. There was a good response to the advertisements. Half the applicants came from the City and business worlds, from people who had done their stint there and fancied that the arts would make a more pleasant working environment for the rest of their lives. A massive drop in salary could easily be reconciled with a significant increase in quality of life-satisfaction. This was encouraging. At the formal interview, the attitude of the majority of these business applicants was less so. All explained in turn that they saw their mission as being to help the arty folks do their sums. It was, after all, well known in business circles that arts people could not add up; fortunately, help was at hand in the shape of people who could. Unsurprisingly, no one who took this attitude was appointed.

That experience – not an isolated one – points to the demons that block the road to understanding between arts bureaucrats and arts practitioners. The new Chairman of the Arts Council of England, Gerry Robinson, Chairman of the Granada Group, lamented in his inaugural Arts Council Lecture in October 1998: 'Some have seen the appointment of a businessman to the Chairmanship of the Arts Council as a threat to the very life-blood of the arts.' True enough, and his lecture did not do as much as it might to assuage those anxieties. But, as he unconsciously revealed in that lecture, his own view of the arts world is peopled with demons of misperception: 'We will no longer tolerate an assumption too widely held across the arts in

* The Arts Council Lecture was delivered in October 1998.

the past,' he thundered in a rather excessively business corporate tone, 'that artistic excellence is somehow a substitute for proper management or that sound financing is somehow too vulgar to be a concern.' It sounds as if a heavy schedule of meetings with arts leaders is needed to show him what a parody of reality that statement represents.

For the tone struck in the lecture is not a happy one: more a lecture at the arts than to them, still less a lecture about the arts. Perhaps a period of ideological disarmament is needed. The arts world will set aside its suspicion that Gerry Robinson regards subsidised clients as no different from loss-making catering subsidiaries – to be given five years to balance their books or shut up shop. In return, he will stop treating his arts clients as innumerate and profligate ninnies with permanent begging bowls as an extension of their right arms.

Yet all is not lost. There is a good deal that the new Chairman of the Arts Council gets right in his lecture. He recognises that the Lottery's 'Arts for Everyone' scheme – otherwise shortened to A4E – was a huge success in identifying an insatiable demand for grassroots participatory activity. Understandably, he places less emphasis on the way that the subsequent call for funding far exceeded the supply of cash available.

Robinson makes well the case for devolution of arts spending from the centralised dispensations of the Arts Council in Whitehall to the Regional Arts Boards. It is the spirit of the times, to be sure. He seems properly realistic about the caution with which the transfers of cash and responsibilities must be handled and the time it will take. Having made a reality of his promise of a 'bonanza for the regions' (to use his words) – with an increase in resources of no less than forty-four per cent in the Arts Council funding round in December 1998 – then the need to make sure that the newly enriched Regional Arts Boards do not spend those resources like drunken sailors moves towards the top of the ACE's own priorities. Judging by Gerry Robinson's words, it reads as if it will. His other comment, about the need to use the Arts Council as a body concerned with strategic decisions – presumably to look at arts as a whole rather than being tied up with particular companies and hard cases – will be tested against performance.

On easier ground, Robinson makes the now familiar and well accepted case for the arts as significant contributors to the physical and spiritual well-being of society. Do you want a distressed urban environment regenerated? Call in the arts. Do you want jobs created? Call in the arts. Do you want healthier patients in hospitals, more imaginative children in schools, a more lively response to treatment from the handicapped or the elderly? Call in the arts. Too often these calls sound no different from the tired old arguments for the arts made by those ashamed to make claims for them in themselves.

A large part of the lecture is devoted to the facts and figures quantifying the economic benefits associated with the arts. Employment in the 'cultural industries' has grown by 34% in the decade from 1981 to 1991 against a mere 4.6% in general employment. (You would of course expect something like this in an economy shifting from traditional manual to thought-based industries.) Artists, sculptors, authors and designers now turn over £2.5 billion compared with £1.1 billion five years ago. Arts related tourism earns £2 billion a year for Britain, a fifth of the entire national earnings from tourism.

Admirable as these figures are, however, they remain peripheral to the big issue of why the arts should be funded at all, and funding the arts is the *raison d'être* of the Arts Council. Mozart is Mozart because of his music and not because he created a tourist industry in Salzburg or gave his name to decadent chocolate and marzipan Salzburger kugel. Picasso is important because he taught a century new ways of looking at objects and not because his paintings in the Bilbao Guggenheim Museum are regenerating an otherwise derelict northern Spanish port. Van Gogh is valued because of the pain or intensity of his images and colours, and not because he made sunflowers and wooden chairs popular. Absolute quality is paramount in attempting a valuation of the arts; all other factors are interesting, useful but secondary.

Still, if these are the yardsticks by which Gerry Robinson judges the arts, they should be welcomed and encouraged. What is not clear is how the Chairman will use the evidence that, like Guinness, 'The Arts are Good for You,' to make the case for increased government funding. His own declared priorities include a readiness to provide a 'more confident advocacy on behalf of the arts by the Arts Council'. We are left to wait and see how and when he does this. To judge by too much of the tone of the lecture, Robinson feels that the arts still need stern admonition – about management responsibility? – before he is ready to move into 'confident advocacy' on their behalf. It remains unclear at the end what the arts must do to be worthy of his 'confident advocacy'. How can we make him more confident?

When he has gained his confidence, what will he advocate? Still standing on the familiar ground, Robinson invokes the Blessed Trinity of 'Excellence, Education and Access'. The last has been so exhaustively and tiresomely worked over that it needs no further discussion here, except to wince that Robinson, in his 'the arts are bad-boys' mood, still voices the trite accusation that arts bodies spend more of their time keeping audiences out rather than getting them in. Education in the arts is now plugged to the point of banality. Yet the fact that he chose to use the Los Angeles Philharmonic as the paradigm of good educational outreach work, ignoring the role played by British practitioners in creating these very programmes at the LA Phil in their early days, was a revealing insight into his reluctance to give much credit to the British arts world. One can only hope that the angry response his lauding of the LA Phil drew from British arts educationists will have helped him to acknowledge that there are good examples to draw from in his own backyard. It is as if it is necessary to give the arts a bad name now so that he can get maximum credit for any subsequent improvement.

That leaves the first part of the Trinity of aspiration: excellence. The arts must be 'excellent'. To be sure. But what, apart from calling for excellence to be achieved, will he do as Chairman of the Arts Council of England to help the arts institutions to achieve it? His lecture leaves that fuzzy. Any theatre or dance company, any opera house, any orchestra, any arts centre can offer a list of things that are essential for artistic excellence to be created. But as he makes very clear, the Chairman is not interested in an 'assembly of wish lists from every part of the arts constituency'. For Gerry Robinson, 'We've seen that before and what a waste of effort it was.' But what about dreams, what about ideals, where is the room for visions, what place is left for ideas? Is there no place for them in this brave-ish new world? Excellence cannot be created without them. Must the arts bodies that create excellence set their visions aside just because the Chairman is impatient of what he calls 'wish lists', preferring 'a limited number of deliverable priorities' instead? Even on his own terms, how do you decide which 'deliverable priorities' you want to concentrate on unless you have dreamed a far longer list first and decided which you want to deliver first? I suspect Robinson is in a quandary because dreams, visions and ideas are unsound, unquantifiable arty language, whereas 'deliverable priorities' are robust, gritty and managerial. But no one has ever delivered artistic excellence through that sort of talk alone.

There is a further linguistic oddity in Gerry Robinson's lecture. In a word that reeks of Old Labour, he speaks of a 'check list of entitlements to the arts each citizen should be able to enjoy'. The very idea of blanket 'entitlements' without a corresponding contribution on the part of the citizen sits oddly with the rest of New Labour rhetoric, in which they are the cause of so much of the problem: too many people expecting too much 'as of right' and acknowledging their responsibility for creating benefits too little. What can these 'entitlements to arts' mean – no one further than twenty miles from a cinema, fifty miles from a theatre, a hundred miles from an orchestra, a hundred and fifty miles from an opera company? Perhaps there could be a subsidised 'arts voucher' scheme, cashable at a specified list of publicly funded arts institutions.

Not that it is clear that this approach to deciding arts priorities will yield anything much but vague pieties of the 'let's all love one another' variety. Soon after Robinson's lecture – in November 1998 – the world marked the fiftieth anniversary of

the Universal Declaration of Human Rights. Close examination
of some of the more obscure clauses – such as those guaranteeing
everyone a job – show how tragically pointless such global
assertions of priorities can be. Urgent they have been, for more
than half a century; but they have proved to be undeliverable.

Another no-nonsense manager, Greg Dyke, was called in by
the government to revise the Patients' Charter for the National
Health Service. In December 1998, after a year's work, the end
result appeared to be the assertion that everyone should have
access to high quality health care; local health organisations
should be efficient; professionals and patients should work
together; and communications should be open. A lot of patients
could have been treated in the time that such a collection of
truisms was cobbled together. Let us hope that the Arts Council's
list of arts 'deliverable priorities' will turn out to be more
practicable than those for the wretched patients, and that they
are informed by a stronger sense of what it will cost to deliver
them.

As my contribution to the national debate that the Chairman
says he wants, I suggest that a list of arts entitlements should
surely include the following: the right to be taught about the arts
at their widest in school and at college; the right to free access to
museums and galleries; the right to affordable tickets for theatre,
concerts, dance and opera; some right to access to such activities
within manageable distances; some right to more than the
occasional annual visit to one of the foregoing. Should this be
dismissed as just my 'wish list'? Or should it be welcomed as
Gerry Robinson's 'check list of entitlements'? Call it what you
want, the question of what either might cost is the interesting
one. Dreaming of entitlements is the easy part. What citizens
should have is a far cry from what the state can afford to give
them.

There are crucial antitheses that await reconciliation. They
surface on the last page of his lecture, when Robinson makes a
heartfelt plea for an end to 'bogus debates'. Like Chris Smith, he
asserts that there is no contradiction between popular art and
high art, between art as an economic motor for society and art as

self-expression for the creative individual. If only this were true. The fact is that such questions are at the core of all the current arguments. Wishing them absent does not make them vanish even if they could. As part of his own contribution to the national arts debate, Gerry Robinson might reflect far harder on how these antitheses could be reconciled. He might also look back at his lecture and ask himself why so much of it is couched in terms that reflect the polarisation, of which he says he disapproves, rather than those that assist the synthesisation of differences, which is what he says he wants.

For, and also worryingly, at the front of Gerry Robinson's mind there is a schizophrenic view of the arts. This is reflected in a glaring contradiction in the text. Early on, he berates the arts for having the patronising view 'in the back of their minds ... the vague hope that one day enlightenment might descend semi-miraculously upon the rest, that the masses might one day get wise to their brilliance'. Yet later in the lecture he states approvingly, as if it were his own contribution to human understanding, that 'the gateway to Birtwhistle [sic] and Cage can be Strauss and Mozart. A love of Betjeman can lead to appreciation of T. S. Eliot and Simon Armitage.' Many in the arts would agree with him, even while being a good deal more reserved about just how the transmission belt of appreciation works. He could have chosen to give the arts credit for having reached this conclusion long before he did, rather than elevating it to just another item in the charge sheet against them.

At the end, Robinson calls for a clearing away of the undergrowth so that a landscape is created where the arts can flourish. Let us hope that the scrub removed includes a number of the prejudices and preconceptions contained in this lecture. Then the debate about the arts that Gerry Robinson says he wants can really start.

11 Why I'm Still Worried About Tony – and Chris and Alan and Gordon and . . .

'So, are you still worried about Tony?' a friend asked me recently. For a moment I hesitated. Deep concern about the Prime Minister's attitude towards the arts had not flitted across my mind recently. True, he had not 'written the arts into New Labour's core script' as we were promised two years ago. On the other hand, he and his family come to Royal Shakespeare Company productions at the Barbican fairly regularly, and in total privacy at that. When in St Petersburg recently, deciding if Mr Putin was a person to do business with, the Blairs went to see Prokofiev's *War and Peace* at the Maryinsky Theatre. On second thoughts, that doesn't tell us anything about his attitude to the arts. After all, Stalin saw *Swan Lake* at the Bolshoi frequently and we all know what he did to Russian art and artists. No, we have to go deeper.

At the surface level, the arts scene in Britain is being physically transformed. From the rebuilt Royal Opera House to the Lowry Centre in Salford and the Walsall Art Gallery, from Tate Modern and Tate Britain to the National Portrait Gallery extension – when was there last such a spectacular renewal of major arts buildings and institutions? The physical landscape for the arts is being transformed. Building for the arts has become intimately connected with urban renewal, social diversification and economic recovery. Surely the arts have found a justifiable place even in the Treasury's pallid and withered sun? Even their bean counters can see a connection between arts investment and jobs, taxes and increased revenue. And that is what justifies arts investment, isn't it?

The rosy panorama stretches even further. There are eleven

good reasons for going to the Dome and none of them is connected with the contents of the Dome itself. Those reasons are all architectural: the eleven tube stations of the Jubilee Line Extension. From Stratford in the east to Westminster in the west, they stretch like a string of architectural pearls, a living exhibition of some of the best of British modern architecture. Had any other country in Europe produced such quality public architecture, both functional and spectacular, then we would all be beating a Weekend Break trail to see them. New Labour's response to this creative achievement was to lament the overrun cost on the Jubilee Line Extension itself – quite rightly – but without ever playing in a positive line about the artistic achievement of the architecture. There can only be one explanation. No one in New Labour's senior ranks – fixated as they were on promoting the vacuous contents of the Dome – thought the architectural achievement of the JLE stations was worth celebrating. Creative Britain was there staring them in the face and they could not see it. As this realisation dawned, I understood why I am still worried about Tony – and Chris and Alan, for they are all in it together. My worries cluster around two aspects: what they do and what they and their supporters say. Let me elaborate.

The first problem lies less in what they do themselves, more in what they make arts administrators and institutions do. In the impeccably orthodox name of accountability and efficiency, they load hapless arts institutions with scores, or even hundreds, of performance indicators and make funding subject to achievement against these indicators. There is no evidence that working under such an oppressive regime of scrutiny increases efficiency much, and actual arts performance at all. Accountability of a sort is delivered, but no test has been made of whether effective accountability could not be achieved with a much lower bureaucratic burden. What has never been examined is the opportunity cost – a phrase much beloved of bureaucratic managers – of loading such dubious procedures on the arts. The suspicion must be that political bureaucrats like the current huge weight of regulation because it gives them a vast degree of control over the arts – power that they are in every sense unfit to exercise – and undoubtedly keeps many of them in jobs. It is simply not in their self-interest to ask whether it delivers better arts at the other end – the 'outputs' or the 'product' as they love calling them – because that is not a determining purpose behind their actions.

A friend of mine working elsewhere in the arts sent me the more than 120 performance indicators that her organisation had to calculate, report on and meet. Maddened by the pointlessness and impossibility of compiling them accurately, she took her courage in both hands and simply made them up. No one at the receiving end noticed. When she confessed what she had done to friends in consultancy they congratulated her: 'Well done, that is what you are supposed to do!'

What Chris Smith and his colleagues have failed to do, despite urgings in private and public, is to lift the dead weight of restrictive and time-wasting bureaucracy from the arts. I do not know of a single senior figure in the arts who would not trade relief from this insistent bureaucratic micro-supervision for a simple deal: 'If I get it wrong, fire me. Until then, leave me and my colleagues alone to get it right.' This is not a matter of increasing personal convenience or removing an irritant, but a fundamental issue of the best and most effective way of running the arts. New Labour's way is over-interventionist, over-detailed, over-controlled – because they have no real vision of how they want to see the arts flourish outside the context of accountability and control.

What New Labour does or allows to have done in its name fits snugly with what it says. Recently a senior mandarin, at the very heart of the New Labour arts machine, told a gathering of London's most powerful arts leaders: 'You had better realise this. If your audiences don't go up, then the Treasury won't fund you. It is as simple as that.' Of course, the question of developing and increasing audiences – or 'customers', as consultants insist on calling them – is nowhere as simple as that and the mandarin in question is far too intelligent to think that it is. But the robust language used – dialogue is a wholly inappropriate word – is characteristic of a general New Labour view that people need to be kicked about a bit if they are to perform properly. Clearly, in Treasury eyes, the arts are particularly kickable.

These attitudes and such language are very catching. There are many courtiers throughout the arts and cultural worlds who are only too eager to echo the tones of 'His Master's Voice'. A senior figure at the British Council in Moscow told me in all seriousness that they would indeed be bringing over footballers as representatives of New Britain instead of the tired old rep company of writers, poets and the rest of the arts *flaneurs*. For good measure, she added that the Council was also interested in persuading the new Russian 'successor generation' to hold favourable images of Britain and proposed doing so by bringing over British radio and TV DJs to influence them.

Quite apart from the inherent idiocy of the idea, the fact was we were in a room full of Russian 'successor generation' intellectuals. They were talking about the things the Russian intelligentsia have always talked about – life, art and politics. The thought that they would bother to talk to a British DJ, or think better of the United Kingdom as a result, was too ludicrous even in terms of the evidence all around us.

Yet we know that this idea came from the British Council's own re-branding exercises, where common sense gave way to subservience before the prescriptions of the focus groups and marketeers.

In a similar vein, the inaugural speech by the new Head of the Museums and Libraries Commission, Matthew Evans, Chairman of Faber, had the instant recognisability of New Labour 'no nonsense' speak. Since he delivered the speech in January this year, the museum and gallery world has put him right on almost everything he said in public and in private. For my purposes, I only draw attention to his ringing declaration that: 'In the great debate between access and preservation, the former is in the ascendancy. I also hope that people and services come before collections.' He cannot have failed to notice that without collections there is nothing to which anyone would want access.

But the autopilot resort to such glib phrases and attitudes seems now to be at the very heart of New Labour attitudinising.

And the creation of ever new concepts for the arts to grapple with continues apace. It is not as if the challenge of dealing with the 'excluded' was sufficient. Now the arts are told that they have to find policies to deal with the 'self-excluded' as well. It is the implication of blame and guilt that is so noxious. If someone rejects the whole idea of say, classical music, then they may be deemed to have excluded themselves from ever going to a symphony concert. That is their privilege, their decision and probably their loss too. The idea that the arts must find a way of overcoming this voluntary rejection and that the responsibility for it lies in their very nature turns the whole idea of responsibility on its head. The thinly veiled message is clear; people reject the arts because the arts are too remote, difficult, elitist, obscure – please tick the appropriate box. The implication is not veiled at all. If the arts are too difficult for people's tastes, then they must change the nature of what they are.

The most flagrant example of New Labour thinking came in a draft document setting out an agenda for culture for the incoming Mayor of London. Its definition of London's culture was revealing: 'A walk in the park, using a library, taking a dance class, going clubbing, Sunday football on Hackney Marshes, going out for a meal, watching Chinese New Year and Carnival, watching a film or firework display, going to a museum, learning to swim . . .' So goodbye, the visual arts and galleries; pack up, theatre and drama and the whole of the West End; drop dead, classical music, opera, dance – New Labour's definition of culture has no place for any of these activities.

Of course, after protests the revised document sings a rather different tune. What is so shocking is that the earlier definition could even have been proposed in a draft. It shows how deep the intellectual rot over serious thinking about the arts has set in to New Labour's intellectual foundations. It is far worse than it was three years ago.

So that is why I am still worried. If ever a government's policies needed intellectual rebalancing, it is over the arts.

Part Three: Actions

12 Art for Art's Sake – Art! for Heaven's Sake

This is my credo. I believe in management. I believe in the bottom line. I believe in the vision and mission statement. I believe in objectives. I believe in the box office. I believe in strategy. And I believe in marketing. At the Barbican we were the first arts organisation to use so-called 'mapping' and 'mosaic' techniques for the identification and targeting of audience groups. But we believe in good, appropriate and relevant research, not bad, inappropriate and externally imposed research. That is the distinction we must insist on. For first of all is my credo. I believe in art for art's sake; or better still, I believe in Art! for Heaven's Sake.

That's it, then? All problems solved? Well, not quite. Because you can't believe in all these things, at least not at the same time or in exactly the same way. Art, like socialism, is about the language of priorities. If we set aside the fact that all too often the first priority for the art world in Britain is plain survival, we can at least agree to put art first. And then we can ask 'what must we do for art to be saved?'

To pursue the religious theme for a moment more; when Christ was asked by the young man what he had to do to be saved, he replied: 'Sell everything you have and give it to the poor.' Today, that is the appeal that the arts world makes to the rich: 'Sell some of what you have and give it to us.' Many private benefactors do just that, both personally and institutionally. They are not obliged to do so. It is marvellous that they do. The arts world should not assume that they will. Britain is a long way from having the notion of citizenship, or the structure of personal taxation, that would create a culture of personal giving on anything like an American scale. But if arts funding is to continue to flourish it will need a variety of sources to rely on and a significant growth in personal giving will need to take place. Whether the Treasury's rules on the taxation of charitable giving will make that easier remains open to doubt.

How positive it would be if some of the higher Lottery winners used their money to help the arts in the places where they live. Since the Lottery started in November 1994, more than seven hundred people have won individual prizes of more than £1 million each, some considerably more than a million. It would be impertinent for anyone to suggest to the lucky seven hundred – and counting – how to spend their money, a windfall that transforms their lives. But what additional pleasure they might have had from sharing a tiny part of their good fortune with others by sponsoring a concert, a play or some other arts activity taking place within their community. Not only would they have supported an important local institution and given enjoyment to hundreds or thousands of their friends and neighbours, but they would have discovered the delights of supporting the arts, in whatever form they chose, for themselves. Perhaps Camelot and the Regional Arts Boards could set up a small counselling group to show interested Lottery winners that they could get real satisfaction, and a warm glow of generosity, by moving in this direction. As it is, they are offered advice on how to invest their money. Suggestions on how to use a small part of it in a socially enriching way would enlighten a small part of the arts landscape.

But while the arts must look for support wherever they can, they are not beggars. Self-help, self-sacrifice have always been an intrinsic part of their lives. So when they ask themselves 'what must we do to be saved?' the answer is at once more simple and more complex. 'Help yourself,' is what it boils down to, and I don't mean in the sense of helping ourselves to money that others – whether in the state or the private sector – have supplied. It does mean helping ourselves by making the best of the skills and disciplines that management and financial tools, mission-statements and marketing ,offer us. But it has to be in that order: art comes first, the skills second. We must not get the relationship the wrong way round, and there are signs that some people believe that the substance of business techniques is more important in the arts world than the real matter of the arts. That is what worries me.

So what is art? Or perhaps what are the arts that we are all in the business of devising, creating, promoting, marketing and selling? First, arts are not entertainment in the sense that a ten screen cinema complex and bowling alleys are entertainment. The cinema complex may well be screening a film that is judged to be artistic, but run-of-the-mill movie-going is far closer to mere diversion rather than anything more profound. (This is not to downgrade film as art but merely to observe that most films watched by us most of the time are not even straying into artistic territory.) Besides, the modern film industry is classically the child of the marketeers. Where is the mass audience perceived to be? Youth. What kind of things do they want to see? Action. What action leaps over language barriers? Violence and disasters. What makes money? Youth-oriented, disaster movies with minimal language content, where a fist or a Kalashnikov are the principal forms of communication. What do you do when you or another studio has made a winner to this formula? Make another one just like it.

The fact that this road, however scrupulously mapped, often leads to financial, never mind artistic, disaster does not stop it being followed. The arts, by contrast, may sometimes be imitative, but they cannot be formulaic or market-chasing in this way — or not if they hope to survive. Their imperatives must be the idea, the original, the creative, the unexpected, the different. Double standards operate here. When an arts centre runs up a deficit of a few hundred thousand pounds, the air is thick with charges of bad management and artistic indulgence. Few attempts are made to relate the loss to the ambition of the arts programming. Yet when a major Hollywood studio loses tens of millions on a single film, this is seen as a necessary characteristic of the industry's search for success. Mismanagement is never raised as an issue.

It should always be borne in mind that the arts have a

different, perhaps inconvenient, view of the way we live and behave. Professor Susan Greenfield, the authority on the human brain, recently expressed concern about two aspects of modern life: the CD-ROM, and our constant search for sensation. Young people now, she argued, press a button on their CD-ROM and get instant gratification. It is, metaphorically and literally, 'in their face'. They are confronted by a visual image; in a sense it is imposed on them. Previous generations had, she asserted, to use their imaginations more. When she was asked why using the imagination was better than immediate access to the inconceivably rich supply of information that the CD-ROM can provide, Professor Greenfield said: 'Because it gives you an attention span exceeding a few micro-seconds. It gives you the power to escape from the present. If you don't have an imagination, then you can't interpret what you see.' On her theory of how the mind works, the arts are an essential part of that process of interpretation, harnessing the imaginative world to make better sense of life around us.

Susan Greenfield then argued that if life is principally directed to the pursuit of pleasure – whether raving, bungee-jumping, chewing – then you abandon the past, detach yourself from the future and, in merely blowing your mind, ultimately abrogate your personality. This is a strong warning from an academic observer of the brain and how we use it. But her observations are central to an understanding of what the arts world is trying to make available to society. They define the importance to society of an activity which swims against the tide, goes against the current of so much of the rest of human social life.

If the arts are not allowed to stimulate and engage the imagination, to connect the present with the past and the future, to provoke reflection, then the purely entertaining and diversionary side of human activity will produce more and more of what Greenfield calls 'flat personalities – those who seek instant gratification, in booze, drugs or violence', because they do not know anything better. On this view, when the arts provide an alternative vision of life to the prevailing one of material gratification, they offer society an essential therapy whose social, never mind artistic, value cannot be over-estimated.

None of this is to say or to believe that taking part in the arts involves wearing a permanent spiritual and intellectual hair shirt. The arts are, of course, intensely enjoyable. But that pleasure at its best comes as the result of some personal attention and engagement, some commitment of time, thought and emotion. There is violence in Wagner's *Ring* cycle: destruction, immolation, not to mention incest, treachery, murder and most of the rest of human life. It takes time to get to the final cataclysm — literally days. It can be a shattering experience, but only because the terminal act of destruction springs from an immensely complex set of human and moral actions which lead inexorably to the climactic minutes of overwhelming sensation. The experience of appreciation involves more than sensation; understanding is at issue and understanding takes time; it does not come and hit you on the head. And it is that steady, sometimes slow, sometimes tiresome search for a kind of revelation that the arts must be involved in.

In short, much of what the arts offer is unpopular with, and seen as antipathetic to, the predominant drift of society. To many, they are just plain unfashionable. That will always raise problems for marketeers. And the big one they have to face is that it is when the arts have been at their most shocking and unpopular that they have laid the seeds for their greatest subsequent successes. Stravinsky's *Rite of Spring* caused a riot when it was first performed in 1913. It is now a standard classic and crowd pleaser. Harold Pinter's *The Birthday Party* was judged incomprehensible by every critic — except Harold Hobson of the *Sunday Times* — when it was first performed in 1957. Forty years ago, Mahler and Bruckner were spoken of as if they were twin composers in style, and united in irrelevance and inaccessibility to the general musical public. Where would the concert hall be today without the regular dose of Mahler giganticism?

Three years ago, nobody advised Clive Gillinson, Managing Director of the London Symphony Orchestra, and Sir Colin Davis, its Principal Conductor, that they should perform the full cycle of Bruckner symphonies on the centenary of his death. They expected to lose money on the project but felt it was an artistic effort worth making. In the event, the cycle triumphed both artistically and financially. Who told John Christie that there was a market for high quality international opera at his country house at Glyndebourne? Who told Lilian Baylis that there was a market for drama and opera among the working population of inner London? In all these cases, and dozens more, artistic success came from a prior artistic perception, not from a marketing strategy or concern about where these institutions should 'position themselves'. Yet an instinctive awareness of the position they wanted to occupy – Christie with high quality performance in select surroundings, Baylis with good value performances for the less well-off – sprang from the basic artistic impulse. It was an integral part of the wish to create.

For many of those who conceived these great projects, marketing as we understand it today did not exist. They succeeded on their own terms. The lesson is surely clear. In the arts, the idea comes first, second and last as the motive for artistic activity. No one is proof against bad ideas or good ideas before their time. But without an idea to start with, the rest is a waste of time.

One of Glyndebourne's recent artistic and audience successes was Peter Sellars's modernist realisation of Handel's semi-oratorio, *Theodora*, first staged there in May 1996. I asked Anthony Whitworth-Jones, then Glyndebourne's General Director, how they had come to decide to do it. 'By market research among the existing audience?' I suggested hopefully. 'No,' he said. 'If we had asked the audience, "do you want to hear more Handel?" the answer would have been lukewarm. If we had said, "do you want to see *Theodora*?" they would have expressed fair ignorance of the work. If we had asked, "do you want to see *Theodora* produced by Peter Sellars, the man who did the controversial *Magic Flute*?" they would have given a resounding "No".' So how did he decide to do it? 'I thought Handel was a good idea and Peter suggested *Theodora*.' Elitist – possibly; authoritative – certainly; right – undoubtedly.

But of course the arts need marketing because what we are doing is comparatively difficult in a society where everything is made increasingly easy. Household chores are dealt with by labour-saving; a good thing too. Can the chore of paying attention to the arts be made easier by attention-saving? Writing in the *Guardian*, David McKie drew his readers' incredulous attention to a proposal that St Andrew's, the home of golf no less, should be the site of a brand new golf course, but one without bunkers. The fact that the bunker is part of the essence of the game, just as snakes are an essential part of Snakes and Ladders, is to be deliberately set aside. The new, modern sensibility appears to believe that bunkers make the game too difficult and families will not have a nice day out if they spend too much of their time thrashing away in a sand trap. But golf is difficult, life is hard and only a fool thinks that ladders are more a part of life's experience than snakes.

At the end, McKie observed that we 'live in a culture which wants to make everything easy, to say: "this is not going to hurt"; to turn sport into showbiz; to take the pain out of politics' – and he might have added 'out of art, too'. 'That is an unhealthy culture,' he went on, 'not least because it denies what many have learned, sometimes painfully, to be true; that there is often deeper satisfaction from things that come hard than from things that come easily.' That observation applies to the arts even more. There are no cheap thrills in art, but there are real thrills. They come slowly, gradually, over years, and as a result of effort. How do you market such an unappealing message, which happens to be the real message of the arts, the core – to use market-speak – of their 'Unique Selling Proposition'?

One of the difficulties in constructing a balanced relationship between arts and marketing lies in the instruments that marketeers use to get their information. Above all the focus on focus groups. The problem with them is that the members tell us what they want in the future on the basis of what they know now. How can it be otherwise? They are bound to express wishes or comments on the basis of their existing experiences. They are poorly equipped to indicate directions in which they might be willing to be led. Focus groups are poorly designed to be useful in showing where people might be ready to be taken by surprise. The danger is that they yield results that confirm the conservative, the anticipated, the existing and the customary. If they concentrate on wants rather than needs, the results will be skewed.

The arts must never forget that taste is led and formed by people who appreciate then deliberately go beyond the familiar. If the arts are to survive they must live in the area that marketing can never predict or marketing inquiry can never deliver. They cannot be defined, tailored, processed and packaged into shapes that are guaranteed to succeed. Neither risk nor financial loss can be eliminated. From time to time, a formula appears – say in music. For some years, the Albert Hall was filled every Sunday night with Tchaikovsky, climaxing with the 1812 overture. Marketing would have been in a seventh heaven. The perfect formula: popular, repeatable, predictable as to cost, risk and sales. Unfortunately, the formula, like all others, ran out of steam and out of audience. It was fun while it lasted but it could not last forever. Marketing could not give it new life; another idea was needed and will always be needed. Without an idea, marketing is just a bunch of statistics.

The revamp of BBC Radio 4 in 1998 was an interesting case in point. Never before had a controller been armed with so many statistics. Never before had so much research been done or been available. Never before had a controller offered fewer reasons for listeners to tune in, fewer thoughts for them to respond to, fewer new programmes other than slight variants on tired old generic, consumer-driven formulae such as gardening, leisure, food and travel. All the changes added up to was consumer research dressed up as ideas for programmes. The resulting network appeared to be driven by reliance on the audience's expressed requirements, not on an intelligent, sympathetic interpretation of their real needs. Of curiosity, invention, intellectual reach across, beyond or through the consumer categories to the audience's needs, there was no sign, and still less apparent inclination to venture into such territory.

This most recent instance of editorial responsibility prostrating itself before the focus groups, of common sense and acquired judgement bowing down before the supposed voice of the people, has proved a fickle guide to programming – which will come as no surprise except to those besotted with such research. Two cases vividly demonstrated how unreliable it is. In the first, 'research showed' – and executives spoke in hushed tones of the expense of conducting it – that the 9 a.m. news summary on Radio 4 caused a huge fall in listening at that time. The research-driven answer was to drop the summary and start the next programme on the dot of nine – audiences would 'obviously' carry over as a result. They did not. Only months later, the 9 a.m. news summary was reinstated in response to listeners' complaints.

In the second example, the same focus groups observed that they enjoyed a radio quiz show at around 1.30 p.m. So the entire 1–2 p.m. Radio 4 schedule was rejigged across the week to give listeners a radio quiz at 1.30 p.m. each day; it was 'what they wanted'. Again, within months, it was clear that listeners did not want this formula imposed on them, every single day of the week, and the project was reshaped. There is a fundamental ideological puzzle here for the marketeers. How can the public in one guise, the focus group, voice a wish for certain types of programming; and then in another guise – that of angry-letter-writer – bitterly criticise the changes delivered as a result of those focus groups?

Clearly, these mistakes sprang from the theory that a programme can only exist if it fits with the answers to consumer questionnaires and into predestined categories. The new Radio 4 schedule was driven by one impulse: if the audience switched off, then there must be something wrong with the programme; if they did not switch on, there could be nothing right in it. Subjective perspicacity, professional acumen, the accumulated wisdom of experience, the ingredients of the editorial and creative process, are pushed to one side, made subservient, judged invalid by the iron laws of market research. If ever a relaunch of a major national cultural and artistic landmark such as BBC Radio 4 demanded a Vision and Mission Statement – those tools beloved of the management men – this was it. It was conspicuous by its absence.

When Gerard Mansell, the creator of today's Radio 4 in the late 1960s, reshaped what was a very pre-war sounding network, he knew all about the available audience research. But above all, he had an editorial sense of what he thought the network needed – and the audience would gobble up. The result of his editorial and journalistic hunch – working with that bred-in-the-bone newsman William Hardcastle – was the innovative programme *The World at One*. It was not started on the basis of data analysis, focus groups or anything else; just the specialists' instinct of Mansell and Hardcastle that this was the right thing to do. Thirty years on, it looks a pretty good editorial call. Research and marketing had very little to do with its creation and nothing to do with its success.

So marketing and the arts have a problem. Let us pose the antitheses in a stark way: unfair perhaps, extreme undoubtedly, but not illegitimate.

Art is adventurous, marketing safe; art seeks the unexpected, marketing yearns for the predictable; art wants the amazing, marketing the comfortable; art is orgasmic, marketing anal. Yet we need both, and we both want to make money; we both want the biggest audiences. We have no alternative but to live together, and to live together in a constructive way, learning from and understanding one another.

And the list of things that the arts want from marketing is huge. Can marketing live up to the challenge? Why is it better at saying what the audience does not like rather than the circumstances under which it might embrace the unfamiliar? Why is it not better at constructing the case against charges of elitism in the arts, especially when they are nonsense? Why is it not better at achieving for the arts the breakthrough to the new wider audience?

The truth is that the arts need to know much more about marketing than they do. They must as a matter of course become proficient in business planning, press and publicity, design and production, and, yes, marketing. But each of these is no more than an essential tool for realising the basic artistic idea, the creative vision. Unless the arts master them, these skills will master the arts and distort them, preventing them from doing what they want to do. These techniques, too, must become part of our arts credo.

For I know that the arts will continue to be underfunded; I know that those who work in them will be underpaid; I know that those who participate do so out of love; I know that those who create do so out of belief. I also know that a society without the arts will be a spiritual desert. In such a Hell, I know that no amount of marketing will convince anyone that it is really Heaven. And I know for sure that if the arts do not help themselves, no one else will.

So, I do believe in the bottom line; I am committed to vision and mission statements; I am driven by objectives; I am devoted to the box office. I believe in marketing, too. Because I believe in the arts first.

13 The Concert of the Future – Seeing Will Be Hearing

In 1996, the *Daily Telegraph*'s music columnist, Norman Lebrecht, pronounced the imminent death of the classical music concert. The sickly patient's decline had, according to this obituary, been brought on by a combination of financial greed on the part of musicians and their agents, the reduction in state and corporate funding and a terminal weakening of the public's 'concert habit'.

Three years on, it is worth re-examining Lebrecht's prognosis, trying to establish whether it was a well-judged or exaggerated storm warning, or whether it was all too realistically flying the white flag of surrender over several centuries of musical culture. If the latter, then it is time to write a long, sad postscript to an experience of live performance that might be summed up as lasting from Mantua and Mannheim to the Concertgebouw and the Royal Albert Hall.

If the classical concert truly is dead, or at best just breathing out its dying gasp, then it will be farewell to the sight and sound of the Brendels, the Kissins, the Schiffs, the Perahias, the Pollinis and their like; to the Sterns, the Mutters, the Chungs, the Changs, the Vengerovs, to Yo-Yo and Slava, to Valery and Seiji, to Claudio and Bernard, to Zubin and Colin and all the performers who have lit up concert hall platforms and the lives of their audiences for a generation.

Put as starkly as that, are existing concert-lovers likely to abandon these artists and the experience of hearing them live so readily? I doubt it. Come to that, are the generations of still-to-be-created or converted concert-goers ready to forgo or to be excluded from such riches of experience of performance and music? I doubt that too, but that is a belief rather than a provable assertion.

Besides, the current experience suggests that, despite difficulties, concert-going in all its varied forms is still alive and kicking. The BBC Promenade Concerts – now globally branded and recognised as the 'BBC Proms' – have successfully transmuted themselves from being a 'mere' music festival – albeit the largest and most varied in the world – into an extension of the British summer season, an event to attend and to be seen at, an occasion for corporate hospitality, a desirable 'positional good'. People who probably go to no other concert in the year go to a Prom because it has become an extension of the 'things to do' in the summer. But first and foremost, when they go to a Prom, the audience goes to a concert, and they go in their tens of thousands.

Skilfully promoted, the Proms have not changed their musical character at the behest of the needs of marketing. They had become a musical landmark, national and international, in their own right well before they became an 'occasion', as a result of sticking to their basic belief in the provision of an increasingly broad and eclectic musical repertoire played to the highest standards. The sense that a visit to a Prom is part of the traditional experience of concert-going does not inhibit people from attending – some, indeed, like it better for the very fact that 'it's traditional'. Yet, elsewhere and at other times, the sheer act of taking part in a conventional performance where the audience sits in silence and the musicians dress in white tie and tails, is said to represent a barrier for those who are not regular visitors. They feel 'excluded' by the unfamiliarity of the event and the occasion.

Of course, not all concerts are full all the time. But it does not follow that because many are less well-attended than they deserve to be, the experience of going to concerts is being fundamentally rejected or will inevitably have to be abandoned.

Yet to debate like this is essentially sterile and backward-looking. It would be extraordinary if a way of enjoying the public performance of music that has been set for a century or more should not change, change radically, and change for the better. There is a debate to be had about the form and presentation of the concert – more or less classical – and it is a forward-looking debate that centres on how artists and performers relate to the audience and, more fundamentally, to the use and adaptation of current technology. Used properly, thoroughly and imaginatively, technology could transform the concert-going experience, and benefit significantly the economics of providing classical music.

But first, how do you connect the artists more closely to the live listeners? How do you close the gap between those on the platform and those in the body of the hall? When the great Canadian jazz-pianist Oscar Peterson came to the Barbican in 1996, the concert began with the hall darkened, the stage empty, and spotlights on the awaiting array of music stands, instruments, chairs and piano. Then a voice on the loudspeaker system asked the audience to welcome the drummer, who walked on to a round of applause. The entire six man band was introduced in this way. As serious performers, it was right to identify them and right for them to be acknowledged individually. But their arrival also served as a steady build-up to the thunderous climax for the arrival of the man himself, Oscar Peterson. He was welcomed as the star of the evening but also as a star surrounded by a constellation whose contributions would be essential to the whole performance. There was something both dramatic and democratic about this walk-on routine. It created the atmosphere; we were part of an occasion.

Imagine a similar practice applied to a symphony orchestra. It could work like this. First, the bulk of the orchestra would walk onto the platform, with an appropriate public announcement of welcome, perhaps referring either to a recent overseas visit or to a recent success elsewhere in the country. After all, distinguished visiting orchestras are habitually applauded onto the platform. Why inhibit the warmth of the response for the home team just because they are familiar? The orchestra's section leaders would then arrive individually or in a group, with their names and the instruments they play being publicly announced. The orchestra's

leader would still have the penultimate solo entrance, anticipat-
ing the climactic arrival of the conductor.

Such an introduction would personalise the orchestra's players,
many of them soloists in their own right, give them added status
and respect, and vastly increase the extent to which the audience
could identify, and identify with, the musicians who play the
instruments and make the sounds. It would reduce the gap
between performers and listeners; it would lower some of the false
barriers without diminishing respect for the activity.

Of course, most orchestras – and no doubt some in the
audience – would hate it. It took Clive Gillinson, the LSO's
Managing Director, some time to persuade his band simply to
turn and face the audience when they took their applause. As a
gesture, this is simple and attractive. We want to applaud them
as well as the conductor and soloist. We want to see their faces as
well as their profiles, to relate to the orchestra whose skills and
verve have just moved or excited us. We want the obstruction of
the raised platform, the sense of them and us, the active and the
passive, lessened even if they can never be wholly eliminated.

But behaving like this also encourages the orchestra to
acknowledge the existence of the audience, thus establishing
another part of the chain of recognition and reaction that could
strengthen and give warmth to the concert experience. Using
this suggested 'arrival sequence' would hugely enhance the sense
of sharing and immediacy in the concert hall. It would be a
small, immediate, practical step to reduce some of the sense of
anxiety or bewilderment that the occasional concert-goer faces.
Faces would be put together with names; names with instruments; instruments could then be more easily connected with the
sounds heard.

But a further step in this process is needed, one which
embraces the latest in current electronic technology. With the
use of television cameras, the entire evening could be transformed and enhanced in a revolutionary way. Once the TV
cameras are installed, the video captured by them can be used in
ways that strengthen the whole practice, experience and public
acceptance of concert-going.

Modern electronic technology has developed very fast. Cam-eras are smaller, lighter, less obtrusive, capable of remote operation and can operate on low lighting levels. In other words, bulky equipment, intrusive artificial lights, high staff costs from using manned cameras, are obsolete; so are the old high-capital outlays on the basic camera and TV gallery installations. The price for a fully rigged and crewed TV facility to provide image quality up to the standards demanded by the main terrestrial TV channels (BBC1 and 2, ITV and Channels 4 and 5) used to run at some £40,000 per hour. The sum per hour for programming a lightweight TV unit to deliver images suitable for one of the new digital channels has fallen to an attractively affordable £6,000.

Before examining the wider uses to which medium quality video transmission or recording could be put on TV channels, the impact of such a facility within the concert hall is worth a thought. Imagine the concert platform configured in such a way that, say, three large, high definition TV screens are built into the fabric of the building, taking into account the acoustic effects of the screen surfaces. Imagine, too, six fixed camera positions for the latest small, lightweight, high definition, unmanned, remote-controlled cameras. Remember, that this will be a hall using only the normal house lighting with no added glare or heat from serried banks of filming lights. The TV presence will be completely inconspicuous.

As result, the transmission, presentation elsewhere in the building, or the video recording of a concert can be done cheaply and without any specific, additional disturbance for performers or audience. It will be part of everyday life, a normal facility, a virtually automatic part of the concert scene – but a huge addition to its interests and pleasures.

The programming of the time surrounding any concert will be fuller, more complete intellectually, more varied visually and will present in the most accessible way to the listener the whole experience of participating in a concert. The aim is to add more information and enrichment to the primary activity of listening to the music. In the following suggested schedule, everything that appears on the TV screens in the hall is also available on screens in the foyers and in a relay room nearby. Naturally, everything is captured on video as well.

The 'Concert of the Future' could be presented like this. From 7 p.m., TV screens carry live a fifteen-minute introductory talk or interview with a performer which takes place on the concert platform. From 7.15, they show a five to ten minute promo about the orchestra, a recent tour, the artists, or material about future events in the hall. This stops five minutes before the concert starts as the audience finishes entering and settles down in their seats.

At 7.30, the orchestra enters, in the way described earlier, with voiced-over introductions and identification by name and instrument. The key orchestral section leaders and leader can be seen in close-up on screen as they take their places in the body of the orchestra. Throughout the performance, the main camera at the back of the platform is fixed on the conductor. How extraordinary that audiences pay tens of pounds to see Maestro X conduct and all they see during the concert is his backside. Using cameras and screens, they would see his face and gestures as they have never been seen by the audience before – as the orchestra or chorus see him. It represents a huge quantity of added value, access and education provided by one technical means.

During the concert, the three screens on stage offer a basic selection of shots to illustrate the music being played. It is not a question of attempting to replicate in the concert hall the complexity of images which are delivered to the home TV set – the concert hall listener does not need them and would find them a distraction. The on-stage screens would pick out orchestral soloists, when it was helpful to know where sounds were coming from – not always easy even for an experienced concert-listener. They would clarify the action on the platform by showing the audience things they might not see otherwise; by drawing attention, for example, to a new theme or to an old one being taken up by different instruments. This additional visual information would remove any idea that there are arcane secrets about who is doing what among a hundred identically-suited players. It would increase understanding of the work in performance and intensify pleasure in the music.

Imagine watching the LSO's principal timpanist, Kurt-Hans Goedicke, subtly, almost inaudibly, impacting his timpani at the start of Sibelius's First Symphony. Imagine watching the orchestra's cor anglais player, Christine Pendrill, breathing out the fate theme in *Carmen*. These are the kinds of intimate moments – there would be countless others – that live TV cameras could open up to a hall audience, and which are only incidentally viewable now by even experienced concert-goers. At the very start of the performance, the screens could show the first page of the orchestral score, offering a subtle reminder that the music is about to start and encouraging even restless audiences to settle more quickly. (You could have smaller screens in particular parts of the hall carrying the entire musical score for those who want to follow it but do not want to rustle pages and irritate their neighbours.)

At the interval, with the orchestra off-stage and the audience having a drink and stretching their legs, the screen presentation would continue. For those who stayed in their seats (and there are always some) the possibilities would be endless. There could be audience interviews in the foyers with reactions to and discussion of the first half of the concert, live discussion on the platform about the second half by the composer, critics, players. It would also offer the orchestra and the venue another opportunity to trail forthcoming events, special offers or other marketing opportunities. Then, after a simplified platform routine for the orchestra's return, more music enhanced by TV presentation.

There would of course be objections from some members of the audience about this style of presentation. There always are. For many, not unreasonably, the visual elements would seem, and would be, a distraction. Using them would not be obligatory at every concert; some orchestras or performers might decide to shun such an atmosphere altogether. But there were objections to surtitles in opera houses for a while until the great majority of the audience made it clear that this technical facility enhanced their artistic enjoyment hugely. The absence of surtitles would be inconceivable today.

I believe that, over time, the attractiveness of the experience to newcomers would more than outweigh any loss of support from established patrons – who could, anyway, learn to ignore the images. It would be a disaster if the existing audience were so alienated that it abandoned the concert hall while the new audience was not sufficiently persuaded to be convinced. But the experiment, or something like it, must surely be put to the test, to see where the tolerances or intolerances exist on both sides.

Such a proposed concert-hall configuration is not inimical to the spirit of the traditional concert; it involves no talking down, no leaning over backwards to pretend that a concert is different from what it actually is; it invites nobody to become artistic mutton dressed up as populist lamb. It does not sell the music, the performers or the occasion short. It offers no false prospectuses about what is going on.

But there is even more to this proposal than clarifying and enhancing the experience of a night in the concert hall. Once the TV equipment is installed, the images captured can be used in a variety of different ways for no extra price. For a start, the sequence of events set out above could be transmitted live to a TV channel, with a minimum of ancillary commentary and perhaps some few extra visual ingredients. While the comparatively restricted technical quality of the pictures might militate against their transmission on a mainstream terrestrial network, they are fully adequate, in terms of cost and quality, for one of the new digital channels.

The importance of such a development can hardly be overstated. Top quality arts performances on video are in desperately short supply in relation to the amount of channel airtime now becoming obtainable in the new digital packages. The arts must have their place in tomorrow's myriad proliferation of TV channels, preferably on more than one such outlet. Technology now permits the performing arts to be as available as sport or other entertainment. Cost is ceasing to be a barrier to presenting our arts wares to as wide a public as possible – and might even make them as popular. Tuning in to an arts channel could be as regular and frequent as switching on any other – except, perhaps, football. It is potentially the biggest widening of access to both existing and new audiences in the history of the arts.

Furthermore the recorded video, whether used for TV transmission or not, then exists as a happy memento to be mulled over at leisure or as an educational instrument. Schools, hospitals, music groups, supporters clubs would be hugely enriched by the steady availability of once-fleeting performances now captured on tape. For the orchestra, too, the ownership of this recorded body of performances would represent the start of the accumulation of a capital base of what can rightly be described as 'product' – something more to show for all those hours of rehearsal and the strain of a concert, and to sell.

Beyond such practical advantages, whether you like it or not the presence and involvement of television increasingly confers a sort of legitimacy on events. To exclude the performing arts from it would be to imply that they were excluding themselves from public esteem. That would undermine the case for continuing public subsidy and bring nearer the death of the performing arts. As I watch the numerous TV sports programmes with football players and managers floundering to say something interesting with a handful of repetitive clichés, I fantasise about a classical music equivalent. The post-concert interview in the Green Room would go like this:

Interviewer: 'Well, Clive, how did it go tonight?'

Manager: 'I thought the boys and girls played a blinder. The team work was wonderful, the attack was overwhelming, and there was no doubt who came out on top – it was Beethoven.'

Interviewer: 'What pleased you most about the playing tonight?'

Manager: 'Well, I liked the way the themes were distributed so unselfishly. No one held onto them too long, each section picked the theme up and ran

	with it, and it had tremendous drive and passion.'
Interviewer:	'Any particular stars tonight?'
Manager:	'Well, you've got to single out Andrew Marriner – what a great clarinettist. And of the young stars, well David Pyatt has got to be the best first horn in any British Orchestra.'

Who could say that such conversations – and such a channel – would not be far more rewarding and real than their football equivalents?

But caution is needed; we should not be over-optimistic. In the recent past new forms of technological delivery of music have not increased concert-going audiences. Very often, they may have created a beguiling and convenient substitute for that activity. Opera-lovers listen to opera on hi-fi CDs rather than travelling, paying and sitting. Even the video of an opera pays off its cost at a single sitting – it is, after all, much less than the price of a single seat. No amount of urging that there is no substitute for the real thing can by itself sweep aside economic realities. A night out is a single occasion; a CD or video can fill a score of evenings.

Furthermore, it is doubtful that the video would have the hoped for and vaunted 'Nessun Dorma' or 'Three Tenors' effect, or the Classic FM factor. Surely, it was once argued, all those who thrilled to a few minutes of Pavarotti giving his all in the signature tune to Italia '90 would become instant converts to *Turandot* and then seamlessly convert to the whole world of opera as a result? If there were any who decided to see *Turandot* on the strength of the World Cup, my guess is that they would have fidgeted before the Big Number came, then been appalled by how long the work dragged on after it, with no reprise to cheer them up.

The fact is that opera is not like dipping into a box of chocolates. It is demanding, difficult; it needs concentration and must be taken on its own terms. This does not make it elitist, it merely restates the awkward fact that those very experiences that are worthwhile are not easily mastered. Most of the great moments in opera, notably those celebrated 'bleeding hunks' of Wagner, are greater in their true context than when removed from it. Of course, Siegfried's funeral music in the hands of a Toscanini or Tennstedt makes an unforgettable impact even when played in isolation. But its effect in its right place, towards the end of four operas and some fifteen hours of music is far, far greater. Conversely, there are a goodly number of operas – such as Bizet's *Pearl Fishers* – where the big number really is just that, and the rest is something of a come-down. One spectacular piece of operatic exposure on television does not remove obstacles or guarantee access. The whole process is more complex than that.

Similarly, the failure of the expected Classic FM factor provides a salutary warning against facile optimism. Many assumed or hoped that the sheer availability of short works or extracts from the great classics, of a limited, familiar and predictable play-list, would whet the appetite of listeners for more and they would trade up from the gobbet of the opera or single movement of the symphony to the whole work and the real thing. Undoubtedly there are some who do, but on the whole the 'trickle up' of classical music listening has proved as elusive and unreal as the much vaunted 'trickle down' factor in free market economics: make the rich richer and their wealth will trickle down to those they employ and the things they buy. Neither has worked and in the case of classical music it has not worked for a simple reason.

Those who listen to Classic FM are not doing so because they regard the station as a painless ante-chamber to Radio 3. They listen to Classic FM because that is what they want. They do not want and may not like whole symphonies or operas or string quartets. They are quite content with fragments, extracts and easy listening. They are not especially curious about what they do not know. This is mood listening not serious listening, something different not something worse. The hope that these listeners would migrate painlessly, willingly and in considerable numbers to Radio 3 was naive to start with and has proved vain.

These chastening examples of failed breakthroughs in popular-ising classical music might suggest that the 'TV in the Concert Hall' idea is bound to end with more disappointment and disillusionment for those of us dedicated to widening and deepening the base of classical music-lovers. I do not believe that it will.

My radical scenario takes the classical concert as it is and integrates television with it in such a way that it opens the doors of the concert hall physically and symbolically. It removes anxiety about the apparently private rituals of the concert, it adds accessible communication about the event in such a way that the performance and the performers are demystified. It will never fully 'explain' a piece of music, it will never make a new work simple. But even the sight and sound of composers – such as James MacMillan, Michael Berkeley, Tom Ades or George Benjamin – talking about their work before a concert might reassure the listener that a composer is a human being, who happens to have exceptional sensibilities and spends his or her life trying to do something desperately difficult but splendidly selfless: communicating human emotion through the organisa-tion of sound.

In November 1998, the Barbican presented a 90th Birthday Concert tribute to the great American composer Elliott Carter. No one would pretend that Carter's music, including the long, fifty-minute work premiered on this occasion, *Symphonia*, is anything but intellectually stretching and complex to the ear and mind. The evening was transformed by introducing that and the two chamber music works in the first half with some five to six minutes of video of Carter talking about his pieces and finally engaging in lively conversation with Pierre Boulez about the rights and wrongs of a conductor ignoring a composer's own markings. The combination of the video and the music produced a very different feel to the evening than the music played alone.

But the clinching strategic argument for going down the road I have sketched out is the absolute need for classical music in performance to regain its place in the universe of the electronic media. The decline of classical music on BBC TV – a few Proms apart – has been as disastrous for classical music as it has been indefensible for the BBC. Music in performance must become a normal part of what the multi-channel viewers have on offer on their screens. Music cannot force its way onto them. But concerts must do everything that they can to remove the barriers – institutional, organisational, attitudinal – that prevent such a process. There is a price to be paid for making this new concert-hall environment possible, the price of entirely new flexibility on the part of musicians and soloists. If the orchestras do not make themselves available by helping to create that environment, then the ultimate price to be paid, of a weakening public awareness of the existence of classical music at all, will be huge.

14 The Cart and the Horse – Which Came First: The Market or the Art?

Imagine that you are the director of an arts centre or arts institution. Imagine that you are having a disappointing season at the box office. Imagine that your grant – if you have one – is being cut. Imagine that your sponsorship targets are contracting. What is your reaction? Call in the marketing department and blame them for not selling the tickets? Ask the press department why they are getting so few feature articles about your work? Quiz the education department about why the next generation audience for the arts has not appeared yet? Demand of the house manager why the atmosphere in your centre is so unfriendly and off-putting? Summon the catering concessionaire and insist that the bar staff are more friendly?

Show me the arts director or administrator who swears he or she has not responded to financial difficulties by doing one or all of these things and I will show you a liar. I go further. If you habitually resort to more than one of these, you should not be an arts director or manager. The fault, dear Brutus, lies in ourselves, not in our stars. The fault, dear colleagues, lies in our arts policies not in the services that surround them.

If things are going wrong at an arts centre, then the strategy is wrong. No amount of press articles, good customer care, corporate sponsorship, educational outreach, or niche marketing can, of themselves, save you. None of these activities should be blamed. There is an old Czech saying about managerial responsibility: 'A fish stinks from the head.' Arts managers and directors are at the head of their organisations. If there is a bad smell, don't look accusingly at somebody else; check your own halitosis.

I put my case rather earthily, because I think we are in danger of being buried under loads of managerial cant about business and business methods that distracts from the essential, the first task, of having an artistic policy of which audiences want to be a part. Everything else is secondary – from selling seats, to making audiences feel welcomed, to catering for whatever their food and drink tastes may be. All these are necessary conditions for success; but they will not in themselves create a thriving and vigorous arts centre.

The one and only sufficient cause for excellence and success in the arts is the artistic policy itself. As the former Director of the BBC Proms Sir John Drummond once said, memorably: 'It's the marketing department's job to sell what the artistic director decides.' What I am talking about is balance, proportion and priorities, not about whether marketing is valuable. Of course it is. But how must it be used to make it as effective as it needs to be?

Let us take the argument one stage further. Imagine an arts centre where public transport drops audiences off at the front door and picks them up at curtain-down without fail; where the car parks are never full and there are no queues as cars leave; where the food is delicious and cheap, the surroundings and architecture spacious and welcoming, the programmes beautifully laid out, the season discounts tempting beyond the dreams of avarice, and every usher smiles and wishes you an enjoyable evening – imagine a place, in short, where 'every prospect pleases and only the art is indifferent'.

Of course, that would not be enough. It is not a ridiculous scenario; it has its attractions; but ultimately it would be a fairly pointless one. The relationship between the service functions and the main arts activity cannot work that way. Marketing the tickets – or press, or customer care – cannot make up for the shortcomings of the arts policies themselves. Only art can produce miracles; and marketing does not need to sell them, they sell themselves. So what can and should marketing do for the arts? What can it not do for the arts?

For a start, marketing and market research cannot devise an

arts strategy, because none of us – as audiences – really know what we want, and most of us are sufficiently mature to take a risk with the unfamiliar if we trust the arts policy overall. Audiences often only like what they hear once they have been attracted by it through publicity and tasted it for themselves. Persuasion and information play their part; but they must have some message to transmit.

Like it or not, arts programming is best left as the preserve of the inspired, benevolent autocrat. History – past and recent – is littered with examples that bear this out. No prior marketing research told Clive Gillinson, the Managing Director of the London Symphony Orchestra, to mount a huge cycle of all fifteen of the Shostakovich symphonies in 1998. (Indeed, at least one music critic told him that it was wrong to do so as an artistic policy.) A brave manager might have mounted a cycle of the symphonies from Number Five onwards, drawing a deep breath as he did so. But in the event, Gillinson, Mstislav Rostropovich, the conductor, and the LSO, were rewarded with big houses for the risk they took, and added recognition from the critics that at least three of the previously rarely played early symphonies were worth taking seriously.

No focus group told the BBC to devote an entire weekend of seven concerts to the work of the Czech nationalist Bohuslav Martinů in 1998, or of eight great concerts to the great French Catholic visionary Olivier Messiaen in 1999. Nicholas Kenyon, then Radio 3 Controller, decided that the time was ripe for a longer, considered hearing of these composers' output, and he had his reward with good houses, excellent reviews and some memorable broadcasts.

Good market research can point in broad directions, can suggest lines of approach, can warn of likely dangers, can interpret matters of style, presentation and image. But it cannot tell the arts director what to do. Focus groups without number cannot answer the basic questions of 'what should you put on to the stage, the platform, or the screen'. They are too small and too personal to tell you much beyond what the handful of people involved feel at the time. They are a poor guide to considered decisions or to likely future behaviour. Atmospheric they may be, well-meaning they undoubtedly are, but they require heavy filtering through the protecting veil of common sense.

The comments of focus groups invite us to lend far too much weight to the individual observations of the members. After the Martinů Weekend at the Barbican, one enthusiastic member of the audience came up to me and said: 'Thank you for such a wonderful weekend. Now please can we have one devoted to Josef Suk?' Another said, 'Well, I know he is overshadowed by Tchaikovsky, but what a treat a weekend of Glazunov would be.' Even experts can get it wrong. One well-known international conductor, after a successful weekend of concerts by Sibelius, said to me: 'You know what we should do next? All the symphonies of Berwald.' I love all three of the composers referred to – Suk, Glazunov, Berwald – but I can think of few easier ways of emptying halls or undermining artistic budgets.

It follows from this that the experience of marketing cannot plan your future programmes for you. Past box office is a poor predictor of future success. Take the task of composing the repertoire of an opera house. Perhaps *La Bohème* was a best-seller last year, as were *Madam Butterfly*, *Aida*, *Pearl Fishers* and *Carmen*. But if they are programmed again and again, or if they are given too long a run in any one season, the harsh reality is that audiences tail away. In our parents' time, the format of overture, concerto and symphony satisfactorily packed out concert hall after concert hall. The answer to concert planning appeared to be: 'Play them again, Sam.' Until that market collapsed too.

For marketing cannot tell artistic planners where to turn next. It did not predict the popularity of Mahler and Bruckner, the former surely now on the verge of over-exposure. The business of discovering that there was a huge audience for the very late romantics was ground out by hard graft, artistic hunch, and commercial daring.

On the other hand, marketing and targeting can successfully maximise a small audience for specialist performers or repertoire of works of minority taste. Some kinds of marketing are excellent at delivering niche audiences for niche products, and for building the core of the audience. I do not believe though that marketing alone ever delivers the full house. That universally longed-for sight comes from a combination of factors, including word of mouth and a sense of occasion, qualities that defy analysis, that defy prediction and that defy the rules of salesmanship. To reach the happy moment when audience demand exceeds the supply of tickets also depends on that special mix of the right programme and artistes, the right advance press, publicity and pricing, and the right marketing. But all the ingredients in the recipe need to be in place. One is not enough by itself.

What else can marketing not do? When it addresses the strategic questions of shaping a new branding policy for a centre, it cannot by itself make an arts institution – whether theatre, concert hall, or orchestra – loved, admired or respected. No amount of changing names, conceptualising logos, designing letterheads, formulating marketing slogans out of mission statements, or other exercises in corporate branding, can give an arts centre a profile unless the institution itself has a real personality. Subsequent marketing and branding activities can raise the profile of the place once it has earned one but it cannot fabricate one where none exists. Only an arts policy can do that.

The reward is to be found when these activities work hand in hand. The Barbican's decision to invest a great deal of time, money and creative effort in a year-long American season called 'Inventing America' in 1998, was primarily an artistic decision. But the way that the idea, those programmes, those artists were knitted into a coherent and captivating set of images and slogans was an object lesson in the effectiveness of strong marketing building on a strong creative theme.

That partnership added a further benefit to what turned out to be a successful season. It was also – though it was not planned for that purpose – a significant step in re-branding the image of the Barbican Centre itself by declaring a strong association between high artistic quality, an immensely varied programme, and a bright, confident image. The fact that festival after festival elsewhere in Britain later discovered the American theme showed that we had caught something in the air before others did.

Marketing cannot substitute for artistic conviction or thought. Like any other management tool, it must be the servant of the core activity – arts. If it is not controlled, unbridled reliance on marketing – or on any other management device – becomes like the sorcerer's apprentice going on and on without rhyme or reason, ultimately defeating the whole purpose of the exercise. An arts director who loses control of marketing and its strategy has lost control of the institution.

These reservations are necessary because the idea is afoot in many quarters that 'if only the arts could market themselves properly, then they would not need to ask for so much money'. If only it were that simple. So what can marketing do to maximise the audience, to ensure that the best devised programming gets the public it deserves? Only a fool would not use every management means in his power to make the arts institution as effective as possible. First the music, then the words; first the policy, then its delivery. How should they fit together?

It is axiomatic that every arts institution should be as professional and expert in all areas of activity as it is possible to be. There is no room for excuses or evasion when it comes to financial disciplines and controls, budget setting, maximisation of secondary sales, commercial exploitation. We do not need outside financial experts to do it for us; we must do it for ourselves.

There are many questions to which the arts world needs to know the answers, or at least about which it needs more information. For instance, research and marketing should be addressing some or all of the following: why do so many members of the audience come once a year only? Is it all they can afford? Is it all they have time for? Is the annual visit to the theatre or a concert like the annual Christmas visit to church? Do they come once and so fail to enjoy it that they never return? Is the performing arts audience made up of a comparatively small nucleus of the professionally-committed and a much larger group of casual visitors which churns between attendance and non-attendance?

The impact of turning each one-time visitor into a second-time visitor on a regular basis would be huge. It would be extremely economical as well. How do we do it? What information do we need to do it? It is often said that turning the single visitor into a serial participant is the key task facing arts institutions. By comparison, winning each new first-time attender is dismissed as being uneconomically expensive.

Well, so it may be. But something about the assumptions behind that revolts my spirit. We are being invited to pull up the drawbridge behind a fairly small gathering of the faithful and to decide that that is all we can afford to do. I think that is miserably defensive. We cannot exist without going out and trying to get the new audience members as well as reinforcing the habits of those already won over. Surely our aim must be to increase the overall pool of attenders as well as increasing the frequency of their visits.

Much is made these days of the idea of exclusion – that is to say, the notion that there is some kind of barrier of taste, knowledge or behaviour connected with the arts that is almost designed to keep out the well-intentioned but uninitiated. My first reaction to someone who says that some activity is too difficult – whether in the arts or in sport – is to reply, 'How hard have you tried yourself?' I would not go as far as Pierre Boulez who replied when asked about audiences' continuing terror of twentieth-century music: 'In my opinion it is laziness. They are not in the habit of listening and do not want to acquire the habit.' Then he added as a comment on those who want entertainment rather than searching art: 'It's like saying that you admire a mountain landscape but then finding that climbing one of those mountains is quite hard. There's no escape from the fact that anything worthwhile may also be a struggle.'

How many arts institutions are prepared to blazon on our mission statements a Government Health Warning: 'Visiting an Arts Institution May Make your Mind Hurt.' How, therefore, can all our best research find ways of bringing appeal to the essential fact that living art is not something cosy and comfortable, but challenging and often disturbing.

When questions of the failure to attract large audiences come up, much is made of the danger that current education policies – in Britain at least – are so geared to passing on information about the present that they ignore the accumulated knowledge of the past. Audiences of the future are not being created by the schools which put such a heavily contemporary focus onto learning and claim that unless something is 'relevant' to children and the world they know, then it will not be learned and therefore should not be taught.

Is it true that the next generation is being disabled from taking part in the arts because of lack of formal education in them – particularly music teaching – and sheer lack of information? It sometimes looks as if the audience of the future is a lost generation, rather like Peter Pan's Lost Boys. But we need more information about the extent of the loss and a better strategy for putting it right.

More important, though, is the campaign that is still being fought by the arts world, with increasing success, to persuade governments that arts and music teaching is not an optional add-on to the curriculum but is an essential part of personal and social education. Marketing might help us here – but the prior role must be taken up by political advocacy and the engagement of the press in a vital public debate. The arts community must deploy every skill it possesses if it is to continue to flourish. Unless we speak up for ourselves and mobilise campaigns on behalf of the arts, no one will believe that we have a case worth taking seriously. Today, every arts manager and director must be a publicist and crusader too. Governments and arts administrators do not like it – they want a quiet life – but the arts gain nothing from behaving like lambs waiting for the slaughter.

The questions to which we need answers multiply. For instance, why are arts institutions – and the media in all their forms – urged to appeal to the youth market as if that market were going to dominate the pool from which we take our audiences? The demographic evidence from one of Britain's leading research firms – MORI – is exactly the opposite. The proportion of young people in the British population has fallen from 26% in 1971 to 20% in 1991 and will fall to 16% by 2021. Naturally, the proportion of the population in the grey or greying category is growing proportionately, and it is precisely the educated and reasonably well-off members of the 'third age' category who are increasing. Haven't people always turned to the more serious arts as they mature? From this pattern, which applies to Europe as a whole the conclusion for the arts world ought to be that its potential audience is on the increase. Why has this part of the analysis been ignored? If we persist in drawing up arts policies overwhelmingly aimed at the youth audience when the population overall is ageing, then we risk skewing our activities and priorities in a quite disastrous way. No one wants concert halls to be filled only with the middle-class, the middle-aged and the comparatively well-off. But they are a potential audience who should not be disregarded in the pursuit of the young. Why are the middle-aged and the middle-class the only segments of society that have no right to protest at exclusion? There are signs that newspapers and TV stations are at least starting to question their own headlong and so far uncritical 'rush to youth'.

It is also often asserted that audiences for classical music are falling, according to some that they are in terminal decline. They are certainly more diverse, more specialised in their interests, and spread over a hugely increased number of performances and venues. Put together the figures for festivals that fill the land each spring and summer, for national and regional orchestras giving performances, and international orchestras visiting, add in the stubborn persistence of London in supporting no fewer than five major orchestras and a vast proliferation of new ensembles, and it is hard to believe that the overall total of those attending classical music performances is falling. Fundamental demand may well be buoyant; but it could have splintered into many more tastes and forms. If this is correct, then competition from differentiated venues and performers is our problem, rather than a lack of interest. Responding to the correct symptom is crucial.

The remedy will be different in each case. But we are invited to behave and act as if the research points to one conclusion only – a fall in demand.

There is anecdotal evidence to back my scepticism and to suggest that it is possible to increase supply and to create demand. Take the Wigmore Hall in London, now recognised as the world's most successful chamber-music and song-recital venue. A generation back, the hall was closed on Sunday evenings and even some weekday nights because the audience – country-home-owning, well-to-do – was simply not there. Today, the 'Sunday Morning Coffee' concerts are sell-outs, and the Sunday evening concerts are just as likely to sell out as the others. The reason is that the audience for such music has not only changed but grown hugely. I do not believe that the Wigmore Hall is the only institution to buck the supposed trend. The Wigmore, under the single-minded artistic direction of William Lyne, has achieved its present eminence, a high point in its hundred-year history, since adopting an uncompromising policy of putting artistic quality first. Its reputation has sprung from its artistic actions. Artistic and financial success have followed. Thereafter, marketing this success, boosting ticket-sales and getting the message to the press were relatively easy. Today, its seemingly effortless association with artistic excellence makes the subsequent needs of branding and positioning easy.

In 1995, the Barbican Centre faced an awkward dilemma when the Royal Shakespeare Company announced its withdrawal from the Centre for six months each year. Some thought it insoluble. We could have washed our hands of the problem and decided it was too difficult to find a substitute for the RSC. Or we could have handed over to a commercial management to fill the gap. Instead – with further support from our funders, the Corporation of London – we reshaped the theatre into a fully flexible performance space. Backed by Arts Director Graham Sheffield's artistic hunch and supported by market research, a programme of international drama, dance and lyric theatre was assembled, unique in London since the celebrated Peter Daubeny

Seasons of International Theatre a generation ago. The Barbican's 'BITE '98' season was a fruitful combination of artistic belief and market research. It was high-risk. It was experimental. It was good quality. It was very expensive. Artistically, it was the only real option for the Centre if it wanted to advance from the situation that it was in. The task of marketing was to present that season not only to meet our box-office targets, but to persuade audiences to come because they understood the relationship between the centre, the events it was presenting, and the standards at which they were offered.

We did not meet our box-office targets. That was not a reflection on marketing but on a very ambitious set of artistic decisions. If there was a budget penalty for our ambition to be paid, we knew why we were paying it. There were alternative rewards. Not least among them was that the season reinforced the process of repositioning the Centre and re-branding it. Long seen as an essentially 'classical arts' centre, it began to be recognised as an institution with commitment to the classical-arts canon at its core; but with a knowledge of the contemporary arts scene in all the diversity of its forms as an essential part of its character.

This process will be taken on in a systematic way in due course. Here, the marketing professionals will play their part in interpreting and presenting to the public in a defined way the manner in which this particular centre has changed and developed. It is not so much that the artistic horse must come before the marketing cart; it is a fact that unless they pull together and in the same direction, neither of them will get anywhere.

15 Don't Shout at a Building; Live With It

Everyone knows the old saying: 'Surgeons bury their failures; architects cover theirs with ivy.' What remedy is left to arts administrators?

Let me make one thing clear. I do not regard the Barbican – the entire complex including estate, arts centre and Guildhall School of Music and Drama – as a failure. The 4,500 residents on the estate regard it as a good place to live. Property changes hands at steadily increasing prices. It is the best heeled estate in Britain per capita. Only the well-off middle classes do not jib at living on an estate these days. Many acquaintances have told me what a good place it is to bring up a family. On a wet weekend afternoon, if all else fails, the children can run through the centre's wide-open carpeted foyer spaces with freedom and abandon until exhaustion sets in.

Nor do I regard the centre itself as an architectural failure. The concert hall, theatre and cinemas are widely regarded as satisfying venues for audiences – the theatre outstandingly so. The particular configuration that puts onto one site all the performing arts as well as two art galleries and three cinemas, allows us to present integrated, cross-arts festivals and events which no other arts centre in Europe can or does manage. Any building which permits such activity cannot be all bad.

However, it is the worst kept secret in London to say that the building is not perfect. We know; we live with its imperfections every day. Every evening, some members of the audience remind us of them. I am not going to rehearse them in detail. But every evening too, outstanding performances are given, outstanding artistic experiences are enjoyed; these are facts too.

Yet there is a tension between what the building is – flawed – and the events that it allows to happen within its spaces – rich and diverse. To understand how these tensions can be reconciled, we must go back to the origins of the Barbican estate and arts and conferences centre.

In December 1940, the site was literally levelled during the blitz of London. The area of the City from Finsbury in the north to Gresham Street in the south, and from Moorgate in the east to Aldersgate in the west was devastated by Luftwaffe bombs. Some sixty acres in all was left desolate. By the end of the war in 1945, according to one eye witness, in an oddly lyrical mode, 'nature has taken over and apart from pig keeping and vegetable growing on an allotment near Cripplegate Church, the whole area had grown wild with, among others, the rosebay willow-herb (*Epilobium angustifolium*), the elephant hawkmoth (*chaerocampa elpenor*) and the black redstart (*Phoenicurus ochrurus Gibraltariensis*) as the new inhabitants. So it remained untouched while less severely damaged parts of the City were gradually recovering and rebuilt.'

Perhaps the sheer scale of the devastated sixty acres was too much of a challenge to remedy. In today's robust, managerial language, it was not long before it was seen as an opportunity.

Certainly, when, in August 1956, the Minister of Housing, Duncan Sandys, invited the Lord Mayor and the Corporation of London to create a residential area, citing a wish for 'open spaces and other amenities even if this means forgoing a more remunerative return on the land', the hint was clear enough. The Common Council of the Corporation took up the challenge and spent the next twenty-six years turning it from a ministerial exhortation into a reality. The arts centre – the final element in the scheme including the residential estate – eventually opened in 1982.

Throughout, the ideas behind the Barbican were ambitious, noble and visionary. According to George Vine, a member of the Barbican Committee for thirteen years, writing in 1974, the intention behind the Barbican development was to bring back life into the City, 'to have a heart of its own, a residential oasis in the midst of the business world of banking, finance, insurance and commerce'. It looked towards other grand pieces of urban layout in London, such as Nash's Carlton House Terrace and the Adelphi of Robert Adam as examples and sources of inspiration. And it was clearly inspired by the more recent ideas of urban living defined and pioneered by Le Corbusier.

Indeed, in a perceptive article about the Barbican written by Loyd Grossman in *Harper's & Queen* in 1982, he specifically related the architectural inspiration of the Barbican's characteristic concrete columns to Le Corbusier's Villes Pilotis of 1915, and of the low terraces punctuated by point blocks to the Ville Contemporaine of 1922.

Grossman is worth quoting on other aspects of the completed scheme. 'It lacks a suitably grand entrance.' We can all agree on that – indeed the architects specifically did not design a clear entrance. 'Arriving by foot is daunting, arriving by car is depressing.' Many would echo those sentiments to this day. Grossman pinpointed the trouble caused by the highwalk system, the first of its kind in London and ultimately the only one. By pushing human and pedestrian activity twenty feet up into the sky, you have what he called 'an unhappy result – a town without streets, theoretically efficient and salubrious but practically bland and sterile'.

He contrasted it with the views of architects, such as Peter and Alison Smithson, and the great American architectural writer, Jane Jacobs, who preached the importance of preserving the human vitality of the town street at ground level rather than the more remote, isolated values of the tower block in the sky.

Grossman was puzzled, too, by what he saw as the very un-English absorption of fragments of architectural history onto the site: the fifteenth-century church of St Giles, Cripplegate, stuck in its brick piazza, 'most un-English and weird'; the fragment of Roman Wall onto which you can only look down, 'an emblem of the past, rather than an integral part of the environment'. Both feel fossilised and remote from human activity in their deliberately managed surroundings.

And yet, despite these criticisms, Grossman was finally won

over; he called it 'ravishing on a summer day' with its lawns, ducks, trees and window boxes. (Today, I would add: with its heron quietly fishing among the fat goldfish in the lake; with the terraces full of audiences enjoying a drink or a meal in the full rays of a declining sun of a summer evening. These are moments of good urban living.) And he concluded: 'It is highly accomplished, it is good architecture.'

Another trenchant architectural critic of the time, Kenneth Robinson, also concluded on an upbeat note in 1982: 'Strangely enough, it is the monumentality of the centre and its immediate environment – the Barbican housing – that makes it more than just tolerable. It is impossible not to be impressed by some indefinable quality about an architecture that is so alien to London and yet now seems so rooted in the site, like the Roman Wall that runs through it.'

Given these bitter-sweet verdicts, how did the final result emerge as it did? Some of it, the configuration of the housing estate in particular, was no accident; it was design, the inspiration of two of the three architects responsible for the complex, Chamberlin, Powell and Bon.

Yet according to the last survivor of the three, Geoffrey Powell – whom I talked to only months before his death – there had been an earlier vision of the estate. It was a very different one, with which Powell clearly had far greater sympathy. The housing was far lower, arranged in more varied configurations, with more enclosures, but a higher density overall. The preferred pattern of layout was the then fashionable ziggurat style, two examples being Leslie Martin's Gonville and Caius hall of residence in West Road, Cambridge, and the Brunswick Square housing and shopping development in east Bloomsbury in London.

I vividly recall a contemporary reaction to Martin's inward-looking ziggurat court at Cambridge, which appeared as a heartening example of modernism when I was up at Cambridge in the late 1950s: 'Undergraduates need their rooms for three activities: working, praying and fornicating. These rooms are unsuitable for any of them.'

Instead of the existing curtain wall effect that we know today, the denser, more intimate but more differentiated first Barbican layout would have been surrounded by a green moat allowing an open view of the site. It would have been crossed from the west by a bridge, leading into a square with water, restaurants and shops. It is certainly an interestingly different vision from the one we have today.

There were other elements to that earlier vision. One – a favourite of both Geoffrey Powell and Frank Woods, who later took over the CPB architectural practice – was the relocation of Temple Bar to a prominent site at the heart of the estate. Another was the reconstruction of the entire Coal Exchange as a complex for music rehearsal rooms in the middle of the Guildhall School. In Frank Woods's view, such an idea would probably be a shoe-in for a lottery project today. When it was proposed, it sank without trace on the grounds of cost.

To be fair to Joe Chamberlin, who has much of the blame for the Barbican's problems laid upon his shoulders, both suggestions were consistent with his belief that the Barbican development should attempt to integrate the modern with the historical in its architecture. Whether imported historical fragments of this and that would have provided a real sense of historical integration, rather than inducing a feeling of fussy heritage theme-park chic is an open question. It would have saved the Coal Exchange though.

So why was there such a dramatic change from one kind of scheme to the one we know today? According to Geoffrey Powell, it was the Corporation's insistence on the application of the highwalk system, the separation of pedestrians from traffic being very much the planning flavour of the moment. Everyone at the time was heavily influenced by Colin Buchanan's 'Traffic in Towns' and the separation idea was a prevailing orthodoxy too strong to be bucked. The need to apply that principle totally altered the style, architecture, nature and feeling of the estate.

But worse was to come. Having insisted on separation in the Barbican development, the Corporation's planners failed to stick to their highwalk principles elsewhere in the City. Finally – according to Geoffrey Powell – the Planning Committee

deliberately sabotaged it by failing to insist on the construction of
a highwalk system on the west side of Aldersgate Steet linking to
the Barbican Station footbridge and directly over to the estate
and centre. The Barbican complex was left dangling, literally,
high and dry six metres off the ground.

To be fair to the Corporation's planners, the entire fashion for
'off the street' developments was waning. It was also clear that
the listing of buildings with historical architectural interest
would have prevented the imposition of a unified highwalk
system on any scale in the City area.

Those are a few of the factors that influenced the development
of the estate, still a landmark to this day and a very popular
example of urban – or perhaps suburban – living. The crucial
thing to remember about the arts centre was that, in its final
form, it was an afterthought. Its development – like that of the
estate – was influenced by shifting political winds and changing
recommendations, not always for the worse.

Originally, Chamberlin, Powell and Bon advised in 1959 that
the size of the residential community on the estate was too small
to 'justify the capital outlay [for the amenity] although a hall
might be provided for the spasmodic uses for concerts, amateur
theatricals, dances and the like'. Essentially, the arts provision for
the estate was seen as a mere extension for the Guildhall School
of Music and Drama. The scale of the proposed facilities –
concert hall, theatre – was planned on that assumption.

In 1963, Anthony Besch, the opera director and arts administrator, was asked if he wished to be considered as head of what
would be called the 'Guildhall Arts Centre'. He declined but said
he was ready to give advice on what the arts centre should be. In
my view, the Besch Report of 1964 is the single most important
document in the definition and formulation of the Barbican
Centre as we know it today.

After talking with a wide range of possible users of the centre,
Besch stated firmly that all the facilities as proposed were too
small for a serious arts venue. They had to be bigger; the Concert
Hall should be enlarged from 1,300 to 2,000 seats; the theatre
increased from 800 to 1,200 seats; both would need a full

complement of backstage artistic and technical facilities to match these increases in size and function. With the expanded numbers of people likely to attend, the centre would need accompanying restaurants, bars and social facilities too. This new arts vision was a far cry from the original idea of an adjunct to the Guildhall School or a glorified village hall for the estate residents.

Crucially, Besch pushed his logic still further. An arts centre of this size would need major resident companies working there on a regular basis – specifically, he pointed to the London Symphony Orchestra and the Royal Shakespeare Company. Indeed, it was proposed initially that the LSO should manage the entire Centre, a proposal that they wisely turned down.

Eighteen long years later, that idea of the two resident companies – and the two he identified at that – became a reality. Thirty years after the Besch Report, those two companies remain among the key pillars of the Barbican's artistic offering. When many still concentrate on the things that were imperfectly realised in the Barbican concept, it is important to acknowledge Besch's vision as being bold, far-sighted, imaginative and one that has been proved right by time and events.

The Besch Report was accepted in principle. Architecturally, the implications of doing so were huge. At a time when the residential estate had been completed, a major achievement in its own terms, the arts centre element was vastly increased in size – indeed, according to Frank Woods, the physical volume of the entire scheme was increased by 150% as a result of Besch's proposals.

It is vastly to the credit of the Corporation that they agreed to them. Did they realise the implications of doing so? I doubt it. The financial implications were indicated, but only sketchily. An annual subsidy of some £80,000 would have to be paid to the orchestra to contribute to an imaginative programme and a further £20–40,000 should go to the theatre company to underpin similar artistic quality. Beyond that, there was a somewhat airy reference to a likely funding gap: 'if part of the financial requirements for this scheme should seem out of reach, a special finance committee should be appointed to consider the means of raising the necessary funds, by private or public subscriptions, donations or deed of covenant from commercial firms or interests.'

It was not what we in the City today would call a robust funding proposal; there is no sign of anything approaching a business plan. But it seems to have been enough for the job.

What would the Corporation of London have said if its members had known that apart from increasing the volume of the scheme by 150%, the arts centre alone would end up costing three times as much as the entire residential estate? As it was, almost half of them were totally opposed to the idea and voted against it.

Knowing what we know today about major arts projects, there is a slightly hysterical pleasure in watching a client doing something that they must not do: changing their mind in midstream. And not just a little change of mind, but a thumping great one. The client has not only had second thoughts but they are bigger than ever and may even be impossible! Only building contractors can read the story and relish every second of it.

With the ambitious Besch specifications before them, the architects took a key decision. A vastly enlarged arts centre had to be accommodated on the existing footprint originally allocated for a much smaller one. This was no time for the fainthearted. Chamberlin, Powell and Bon declined to sacrifice any of the estate's open spaces to accommodate the cuckoo-like expansion of the arts centre. In truth, had they done anything else, they would have had to modify the entire scheme, an even more unrealistic option. That left only two directions in which to go – up and, chiefly, down.

So they dug a hole, 400 feet by 250 feet in area and ultimately 80 feet in depth. The consultant engineers, Ove Arup and Partners, warned Chamberlin, Powell and Bon that if they dug this pit too fast, the already completed huge, residential tower blocks of Cromwell and Shakespeare Towers would slowly sink into the ground – perhaps not so slowly either. They dug stage by stage, and at each stage put in place retaining walls to keep the foundations of the tower blocks stable. This retaining work alone took four years to complete. By then, the early 1970s, the first great oil shock struck and with it the worst inflation seen in Britain in the post-war era. The costs of the arts centre rocketed. Geoffrey Powell recalled that the Corporation understandably considered calling off the whole project. They even contemplated filling in the entire excavated hole with gravel dredged from the North Sea. But when it turned out that this would be insanely expensive, they decided they had no alternative but to soldier on. (This was not the only occasion when the Corporation wondered if total closure was not the best way out of the Centre's problems and costs.)

What are the lessons of this extraordinary story so far? First, that there was no 'owner' of the project, in the way that 'ownership' is understood today. It is no disrespect to the Barbican Centre committee to say, as Frank Woods does, that they were neither qualified, equipped nor inclined to act as a modern owner of a project should. Nor was it part of their formal remit.

But if they were not 'the owner', who was? Answer: the architects themselves. They were the people with the greatest interest in the scheme, rather greater than those who were paying for it.

The second lesson is that there was no architectural competition for the scheme. Chamberlin, Powell and Bon were appointed because of their success with the nearby Golden Lane housing development. Third, that if ever a client changed his collective mind about a project in midstream, it was here. Usually this is a formula for costly disaster, regrets and recriminations. So it has been in the Barbican's case.

It may sound churlish to make these observations, for if the Corporation had not accepted the Besch proposals, I could not have become managing director. But no one can live in the Barbican, still less manage it, without being brutally honest with themselves about such realities. It has been said that the Austrians acquired the Habsburg Empire in a fit of inadvertence;

I sometimes think that the Corporation acquired the Barbican Arts Centre in similar way.

But the fourth lesson of the way the key decisions were taken was the most crucial. For they determined the way the arts centre was laid out and configured. Everything about the Centre for good or bad that exists today derives from those decisions. It is the architects' considerable achievement that a marvellous theatre and a good concert hall, not to mention an art gallery, three cinemas and assorted conference facilities, were shoe-horned onto a site that could not accommodate them comfortably on any conceivable surface plan.

But there was a price to be paid for this act of compression or concentration. The space remaining was far too odd and at too many levels to produce well-articulated public spaces that would let audiences know where they were, how they could get to where they wanted to be, and could feel easy and comfortable in the process.

It was certainly high-density development, or as Chamberlin, Powell and Bon themselves revealingly put it in 1967, the theatre, hall and cinema are all 'suppressed underground'. Today, we can see that it is the very density of the artistic development that has allowed the Barbican to develop what it started to do from the beginning, namely to mount ambitious integrated cross-arts festivals which no other arts centre can conceive or undertake. But all that had to be learned.

The process of learning to live with the building began from the early years – with the ambitious and brilliant Scandinavian Festival 'Tender is the North', in 1985, and has continued to this day with 'Inventing America' in 1998 a recent example. These activities are all part of the continuing process of releasing the building's suppressed energies. Suppressed they may be; but the energy available for release is real enough too.

For the first decade of the project's construction, there was no true owner, in the technical sense. In 1970, the arts centre got one. Henry Wrong was appointed Managing Director and Joe Chamberlin and Christoph Bon in particular soon discovered that they were now dealing with a demanding one – someone who had to make the arts centre work artistically, practically and – not least – financially. More changes were to come, notably the insistence that there had to be a far larger provision for commercial activities if the Centre was to contemplate paying its way. These and other issues clouded the relationship between Henry Wrong and the architects in an entirely predictable way. Yet it does not take much to argue that the presence of a strong owner was long overdue and in many ways – not least the insistence on a significant commercial element in the scheme – Henry Wrong was shown to be right in demanding what he did both as 'owner' of the project and its ultimate user.

The kind of disputes Wrong had with the architects were strikingly clarified for me in a conversation I had with Christoph Bon, not long before his recent death. I put to Bon a question that has often been put to me: 'Why is there no front door to the Centre?' It was clear that he did not understand the point of the question. 'But there are many ways in,' he replied. 'If you come by car then the front door is at the lower roadway. You leave your car, you get into the lifts, go up and appear in the enclosed waterside area. That is the front door. If you come by foot, you walk in over the highwalks and then you too reach the inner waterside area.'

This is not an ignoble vision. I know of two distinguished British architects who approached the Centre over the highwalk for the first time recently, stood at the top of the double flight of steps looking down at the waterside and were delighted by the sense of intimacy and enclosure created by the architectural ensemble.

For many others it does not work because it does not address – indeed, did not want to comprehend – the needs and wishes of the audiences. That is one of the consequences of allowing the architects to have too much control over the project. But then, as Henry Wrong observed to me: 'The architects always said we are right and people will accept what we have done.' That explains a lot. Today, we have to live with the consequences of such attitudes. Audiences do not accept what has been done.

Somehow, there has to be an artistic compensation for the failings of the physical experience in the Centre.

So how is it done? The first thing to remember is that the Barbican is organic. This may seem a wildly inappropriate adjective to apply to a building of such rigid concrete immobility. Yet the idea of a developing organism is the key to the Centre's own past and future development and to its impact on the surrounding areas.

My first thought is that a building is like a person; none of us is perfect. Each one of us has to live with our own imperfections, not to mention those we either don't notice or dare not own up to. We accommodate and adapt to our friends' and colleagues' imperfections. We don't say, 'I don't like your behaviour, let's rebuild you.' We would be shocked if a colleague – or partner– said that to us.

There is, however, a tendency to take that attitude with buildings, too often for non-architectural, non-functional reasons. If an organisation does not work perfectly, knock the building in which it exists about a bit. It is an expensive remedy. But it is often easier to blame the bricks and mortar – or concrete in our case – when the true remedy may well lie in the structure, organisation and internal culture.

I do not believe that the remedies to the Barbican's problems are primarily architectural. That is not to say that some comparatively minor structural adaptations are not necessary and would not have a noticeable impact. Geoffrey Powell told me about the model of the estate that the architects presented to the Barbican Committee. It was in white board. Quite usual. As the estate and centre were revealed, Committee members looked at the bare concrete and said: 'Where is our lovely white building?' There was no point in saying that the model was about the layout and structure and not about the detailed finishes.

His view then, and today, was that the external concrete piers should have been painted white, though both Chamberlin and Bon regarded any suggestion of painting concrete as an assault on their integrity.

Similarly, the attitude to the inner roadway, the main car-borne access point, was revealing. The architects called it the 'Drop Off Point'. They were fooled by their own description. The carriage trade – apart from a few of the very rich or diplomats who really are dropped off – does not exist. The great majority of car travellers 'drop off' inside the car parks; the pedestrian access from the car parks to the centre itself was and remains, and I agree with Powell, 'awful'. We need an architectural solution here.

As Henry Wrong points out, because the estate has no street frontage, and because of Christoph Bon's views, there was no front door to the Centre, no clear identifiable street entrance, and therefore no welcoming way in. I have to say that we have been round this problem twice in my short time at the Centre and it is quite clear that only an architectural solution of some kind will address this one as well.

But look at what has been achieved within the Barbican, despite its physical shortcomings. The concert hall as a perma-nent home for a resident orchestra – the London Symphony – was intended to allow the players to develop as an orchestra because they would learn to live with the sound of their own hall. Audiences would develop greater loyalty to the orchestra and to its home. It has been a major success, with the LSO now recognised as one of the top half-dozen orchestras in the world and clearly the best in Britain. Their artistic programming is adventurous, their sound is sumptuous, helped by some modest acoustic, but non-structural, improvements to the hall.

The theatre remains one of the best designed theatres in Europe. It combines intimacy with the possibility of grandeur. The finest compliment to it was paid by the theatre director Deborah Warner. In 1997, she was due to direct Britten's *The Turn of the Screw* in the theatre for the Royal Opera. Warner had worked in the theatre before but she had never seen the stage stripped bare to its walls before. This was because we had just finished five months' work on the theatre – some of it structural – to adapt it from a purely drama house to one that could take lyric theatre and dance. Deborah took one look at the huge wide-open spaces of the stage, gazed up at the imposing fly-tower, the highest in Europe, and said, 'I don't need a set. The stage is the set.' Her achievement was to recognise that in the deep, distant recesses of the theatre's open spaces, she could create the psychological oppressiveness and claustrophobia that lie at the heart of Britten's opera. It remains one of the landmark operatic productions of recent times.

In the almost twenty years that the RSC have based their London presence with us, they have become the world's leading international theatrical company, expanding their operations to residencies in the English regions and the United States. More importantly, the Barbican – as a building – revealed its true capacity to be flexible and adapt to new circumstances when the RSC decided to limit their London operations to twenty-six weeks each year.

Most outsiders told us that we were stuck with an insurmountable problem. The theatre had been built for the RSC. We had to lump it – we could not fill the empty twenty-six weeks in any other way. It was a classic example of tunnel vision, of assuming that a building – especially one such as the Barbican – can do only what it was initially built for.

We refused to be stuck in such thinking. By adapting the theatre in the way I mentioned earlier – at moderate capital cost of less than £2 million – we mounted an entirely new international theatre season, the 'BITE' season, which added to London's theatrical riches, transformed our own artistic and public profile, and drew in audiences that had not previously been to the Centre. Such a radical change was possible because the basic structure of the theatre as a building was sufficiently flexible to allow it.

Now we come to the problem areas, the foyers, or 'people spaces' as we prefer to call them. I have already spoken of the vertical compression of the building as being the main reason for the difficulty many have in finding their way around. Those decisions, taken thirty years ago, mean that once the enlarged volumes of the hall and theatre had been accommodated, the space between them, though quite extensive, was impossible to lay out in a clear and comfortable way. The public spaces were simply what was left over after everything else had been put in.

Through a process of trial and experiment, we have found that the 'people spaces' are a fine activity area in their own right. With room for an informal performance platform in the foyers, audiences can look onto it and down at it from two levels, use two levels of catering points and bars, and have space to move around, and enjoy whatever other facilities have been provided.

These spaces come into their own during the themed weekends – Mexico, Colombia, Ireland, Bangladesh, Brazil and, perhaps above all, Cuba – that have become a regular feature of our programming. With a changing population of between 1,000 and 2,000 people milling through the spaces, they work, they are enjoyable; they are an incredible addition to our ability to introduce variety of activity, forms and subject matter into our artistic offering. They change our profile to the outside world; they bring in entirely different audiences; they demonstrate diversity, curiosity and originality. On these occasions, no one says they are lost; they are where it is happening and they feel good.

Such experiences do not diminish the continuing concerns of evening visitors but they put them into a wider perspective. They certainly demonstrate that even supposed problem areas in a building can be turned into strengths if you are ready to think constructively. Don't shout at a building, listen to it.

Over the last four years, we have spent a good deal of time trying to understand the building, listening to it, as a prelude to clarifying it for others. We have reached some tentative conclusions.

It is not like an airport which has only two principal functions, coming and going. The Centre has dozens of functions and hundreds of different events; communication and navigation are inevitably much richer and more complicated than in an airport.

Could it be like a department store, which sells a broad variety of goods and needs to provide an elaborate system of direction-finding to indicate the department of the customers' choice? Everyone expects to spend time finding what they want in

Selfridges and Harrods and expects to take time getting there. Why not the Barbican? Perhaps the answer in this case is that the routes of access and communication in department stores – lifts and escalators – are always clear and highly visible.

Or, more radically, should it be understood less as a building, and more as a continuation of the city urbanscape? The notion of trying to comprehend the Barbican in this way came from two students at the Royal College of Art as part of a degree project on the perennial problems of navigating the Centre. They argued that the nature of a building invited the individual to expect to understand it the moment they entered; or that at least it should become understandable within a fairly short time. In the case of the Barbican, they argued, you should look at it less as a failed building, more as a continuation of the urban street scene. For instance, Soho and Clerkenwell are complicated and varied, but their characters as districts and the pleasure you get from going to them derives from the fact that you do not know what is around the next corner until you find it. With time, you become familiar with and recognise the landmarks, and the combination of variety, unpredictability and acquired familiarity provides the pleasure of a typical urban quarter.

The RCA students' suggestion was that the signposting arounding the Barbican had to be more like the signposting of streets and discrete destinations (the concert hall), rather than the expected comprehensive signposting of an airport or a department store.

My own conclusion from this continuing process of trying to understand the Barbican while we change what goes on inside it, is to underline the essential nature of the 'organic' approach. For the organic impact of a building extends to the areas beyond its own walls. It would be foolish to claim that the existence of the Barbican alone has had a direct effect on what has been built on its fringes. These perimeter buildings have changed beyond all recognition in the last twenty years. Probably not even their architects know how much, or how little, they were influenced by the presence of the Barbican Centre.

Beyond the immediate fringes of the Barbican, the economic

and social forces that have transformed St John Street and Clerkenwell as a whole into a thriving, energetic and altogether desirable 'quartier' of London are many, various and only dimly connected with the existence of the Barbican. But the Barbican plays its part in these shifts of habit and perception. Tower blocks are back in fashion with the trendies, though whether, as Loyd Grossman suggested to me, this is due to 'heartfelt rediscovery or merely perverse radicalism' is a good question, though he suspects it is the latter rather than the former. But even a fashionable 'yes' vote based on perverse radicalism is better than nothing.

Closer to our own front door, a vision of the future is emerging organically and it owes itself entirely to the existence and activity of the Barbican. This is how it might look in five years' time.

Less than six hundred yards north of the Barbican, in the continuation of Whitecross Street, stands the ruined church of St Luke's. This will become a rehearsal and education centre for the London Symphony Orchestra.

Just round the corner from the Barbican and less than two hundred yards away in Chiswell Street, the City University Business School, including the Faculty of Arts Administration, will move into new premises in just three to four years.

Scarcely two hundred yards away from our own front door in Silk Street, there could be a major new facility for the Guildhall School of Music and Drama, including a new concert hall, studio theatre and TV studio.

If all these three are built, and two of them are near certainties, with plans and funding in place, you will have, in effect, an arts campus within the square mile pivoting physically around the fulcrum of the Barbican, and increasingly interrelating in a series of functions and activities.

Imagine some of the surrounding streets becoming paved and pedestrianised, with cafés, bookshops and other social meeting points associated with arts and campus life growing and flourishing. Add another element to the urban mix, that of our City neighbours, some of the biggest players in the City –

Linklaters and Alliance, Slaughter and May, Merrill Lynch – and you have the potential for a district of quite extraordinary vitality, energy, variety and creativity. Apart from anything else, it would urbanise the rather suburban temperament of the Barbican estate and would be entirely in keeping with the Corporation's vision of returning life and activity to the City areas.

None of this has happened solely because of the Barbican. Yet some of it has. Much of it can happen on a bigger, more effective scale because the Barbican exists. It was not part of the original scheme of things. But the vision that first drove that scheme now continues to allow other things to develop and grow – organically.

Isaiah Berlin once said to me: 'You will never make the Barbican loved. Oh no. But you can make it respected.' As a building it certainly deserves the effort, not least because it has a lot of growing to do.

16 The A-to-Z of Running an Arts Centre

I f anyone asks whether running an arts institution is a hard job, be it an orchestra, a gallery, a museum, or something that embraces all these activities such as an arts centre, the only honest answer is to say that it is as easy as learning the alphabet – but a new fuller one. The time is long gone when running a concert hall was mainly about programming the music, heading a gallery was chiefly about the paintings on the walls, directing a theatre company was principally about that – directing plays.

Running the arts is more like a business than it ever used to be. In some respects, it is even more complex. On top of the routine financial disciplines that are demanded as a matter of course and necessity, arts organisations work in fields where forecasting audience-response to the artistic programme is notoriously difficult. Tastes change; taste can be shaped; taste needs to be led. Predicting audience response to the artistic offering is hazardous. Eliminating risk is impossible; often the safe conservative line in artistic provision is the most risky. The middle of the road – whether in art or in walking – is the place where you are run over. Nothing is as old hat in the arts as last year's proven winners.

So, how is the basic question to be answered? Is running the arts difficult – that is to say as complex as a business – or is it really as easy as ABC? Perhaps reciting the alphabet will give us the answer to the question.

A is for Audiences and Access and Accountability and, yes, I almost forgot, the Arts. I put the word 'audiences' in the plural – there are dozens of distinct arts audiences, many separate ones for classical music alone. Sir John Drummond, when Controller of

BBC Radio 3 and Director of the Proms, always said that the Radio 3 listeners were composed of dozens of groups who passionately loved one kind of music and – more importantly – loathed the others. Yet, particular as their range of tastes may be, audiences are united by a shared enthusiasm for, and a common commitment to, the arts as a whole. That commitment distinguishes them from their fellow citizens who find no interest in or draw no comfort from artistic activity of any kind. It certainly does not make arts supporters better; it does mark them off as different.

Access is a comparatively new concern. It means more than finding your way around a building, though as I know from bitter experience at the Barbican, that is not a small issue. 'Access' has the precise connotation of extending the social range, the ethnic variety, the class cross-section of your audiences. The arts, we have been told, are exclusive, or at least are perceived as such. A slippery word, 'perceived'. It can lay any accusation against you without providing solid evidence for the charge. So, if anyone 'perceives' the arts as being exclusive, then they have no choice but to try to remove that (perceived) view. If audiences are kept out because they 'feel' excluded, then it is up to arts institutions to change that feeling. In actual fact, any worthwhile arts organisation is desperate to widen and deepen its audience base. Enabling access for each and every one is only a means to a common goal, that of more people coming to and enjoying the arts.

A is also for Accountability. To whom? To those who provide the money to fund the arts, for sure. It is good manners to say 'thank you' in any case, not to mention common sense. Currently, the word holds a somewhat technical meaning: that of answering for your actions to as wide a constituency of people and institutions as possible. To those who ask why you do what you do, you should not only have a good answer, but offer it without complaint or reservation. The call for accountability reflects a need for the arts to tell society more actively why they act as they do, why they spend as they do. It invites the arts to be more persuasive, more open about their beliefs, more bold in their justification, more ready to engage in debate, more eager to confront questioning.

And yes, A is for Arts. 'What is art?' as the questioning Pontius Pilate might have asked, and he would not have stayed for an answer to that question either. If my own answer is not clear by the end of this alphabet, then I have more than a letter missing.

B is for Box Office and Backstage and Business Plan. Take your box office, its head and the staff very seriously. The box office both sells the tickets, and sells the idea of the institution. Its staff represent the place over the phone, and even more so face-to-face. A mishandled phone enquiry can lose a sale in the first few seconds; should the call take minutes to be answered, it can be lost still more quickly. If you ring another venue's box office, you can tell instantly what that place is like. Seen like this, the box office is not only your public face but it proclaims how warm a heart you have.

Backstage are the staff who interact with your artists. Why should international or national stars return to your centre if the treatment they receive backstage is anything but expert, friendly and helpful? The staff may be 'backstage' to the audience but they are face-to-face for the artists. A Green Room which does not feel welcoming, worse, one which is positively off-putting, will make it difficult for artists to perform at their best. They could judge you and their whole experience not by the cheers of the audience but by the glowers of your backstage staff.

B is for Business Plan. The arts world is full of ideas. People like working in it because it thrives on ideas. Sorting out the good from the bad, the clever from the barmy, the original from the merely wacky, is tricky. One useful discipline is to insist on a business plan for any proposal. It will not tell you whether it is a good idea as such, but it will identify just how financially precarious it will be and it will certainly make it clear if you are likely to lose your shirt on it. (More about risk later.)

C is for Customers and Consumers and Communication and Commercial Activities. Oh and Catering, too. Are customers different from audiences? Well, you certainly want their 'custom'.

You always have. So, why change the noun? I do not know, but I have good grounds for being suspicious. Was it mere accident that when the railways changed from treating travellers as passengers to calling them 'customers', the service immediately got worse?

Those who come to the Barbican are certainly our customers. But when they go to a concert or watch a movie or go to the theatre, they have always been the audience, for the very good reason that they come here to listen. The word describes their attendance very precisely – they have come to listen, to attend, to participate. To reduce this rich, complex human activity – that of being an audience – to a mere commercial transaction – that of being a customer – is to diminish both the activity, the artists who provide it and the people who value it. (Of values, more later.)

Oddly enough, I mind the idea of 'consumers' far less. As audiences are to art, consumers are to entertainment. Come to that, I often say that I 'consume' art in the sense that I thrive on it. But if the act of consumption is less rich in a philosophical sense than the experience of being part of an audience ('consumption' after all has overtones of being more casual, less intense, less highly regarded), it still remains a more collective human pastime, usually devoted to shared enjoyment and therefore ranking some levels above the commercially reduced business of being regarded as a mere customer. So my own hierarchy of values runs, from the best to the less good: audience, consumer, customer.

C is for Communication. Telling your staff what you are doing, what the arts institution is doing, is an essential part of management. Either you communicate directly and openly, or the grapevine (at its best) or the rumour machine (at its worst) will do the job for you. Taking and keeping the initiative in the communication campaign is crucial for another reason. If management does not do it, the unions will do it for you. There is nothing wrong with the unions; but they transmit their message and not yours. But communication is a two-way process: it does not merely flow from the top down. There must be ways of having it flow back from staff to managers and management must show that it listens to what is being said.

C is for Commercial Activities. There is hardly an arts venue of any kind which does not sell its time, its space or its facilities to outside interests. We are all rooms for hire these days. But there is a great fantasy abroad: that you can fund the arts programmes by being sufficiently commercial in your exploitation of the buildings and facilities. This is an illusion. The Barbican was opened in 1982 on the confident assumption that its commercial activities would pay for the arts programming. Sixteen years on, the Corporation of London is still funding the centre to the extent of some £23 million a year in operating costs. Without our commercial activities – ranging from catering to car parks to retail to conferences and trade exhibitions – that subsidy would have to be still larger. So while they are a necessary part of the economy of an arts centre, they will never provide a sufficient source of finance to run one in its entirety on any scale.

And talking of which, a vital ingredient of these commercial activities is Catering. Like Napoleon's army, an arts institution marches on its stomach – or rather on everyone else's. Of course the notorious Victoria and Albert Museum advertising campaign that it was 'An Ace Caff with a Museum Attached', showed just how wrongly you can present a message. The museum or concert hall or theatre must always come first. But the fact is that catering does matter. Eating out is an increasing part of social life and for some people a principal form of entertainment. If arts venues do not provide food in a variety of settings and price levels, someone else will do it for them and pocket the profit. Retailers call it the 'Total Entertainment Offer'. We neglect it at our peril. The food which an institution provides tells the audience something about its values.

D is for Discounts and Disabled. The business of juggling with seat prices to attract more audiences is more than a commercial transaction, it has become an art. Judging the level at which the bargains are set, the time of week or day that the reductions are available, the frequency with which they are offered, can make a vast difference to your cash take and cash flow. Beware! Audiences have become extraordinarily canny and price-sensitive. The idea that arts audiences are all flush with cash is a shallow assumption based on broad ignorance of the people who really patronise the arts. They need to mind their pounds; they know what reductions are on offer and when they are available. They will hold off buying until the discounts kick in. Excessive discounting may fill the house, but it may empty the till at the same time.

D is for Disabled. Allowing the disabled to use the facilities as easily as if they had no disability is now an automatic expectation of any arts institution. From wheel-chair access, to convenient seats for those accompanying them, to induction loops for the hard-of-hearing, there is a long agenda of action points that have to be met before equality of provision can be claimed. The solutions are not only technical. Staff attitudes also determine whether the disabled feel a true part of the valued audience or just an inconvenience that must be accommodated. Are the disabled included in more than just a physical way? Awareness of their needs has grown faster than the ability of older buildings to adapt to them. The cost of adaptation is huge. The resources for it often do not exist. Sooner or later, the age and inflexibilities of a building will not be accepted as an excuse for sub-standard disabled provision. Reconciling the need with the inability to pay for it is a looming roadblock on the way ahead.

E is for Education and Excellence. Every arts institution should have its own education programme. Most do. They are not set up as a pleasant add-on; they are an integral part of the activity of opening up what the arts do to people of all ages who have had little opportunity to learn about or to experience them. Whether the education programme takes the basic art forms out to schools, or brings schools and groups into the building for a closer, more intimate involvement with the art in question, or whether the centre initiates arts activities with whole communities, the aim is the same. Education breaks down barriers, opens minds and doors, expands understanding and enjoyment. As much as anything else, it shows that the arts do not inhabit an ivory tower.

Two practical observations. Sponsors like educational projects; grant-giving bodies insist on them. One blunt truth. All the combined activities of every arts body in the country cannot make good the shortfall in the teaching and experience of the arts that the schools once gave but of which they provide less and less. One unpopular observation. An education programme in an arts institution cannot substitute for a part of the national schools budget. It is concerned with bringing audiences into the arts in larger numbers. Some arts education purists dispute this.

E is for Excellence. We are all supposed to be Centres of Excellence. To state that is to state the obvious. Who, after all, sets out to run a Centre of Mediocrity? At least the commitment to excellence signals to all that however experimental or occasionally esoteric arts activities may be from time to time – as distinct from being mainstream, conservative and predictable – they can be embraced as excellent on the grounds of their basic conception and intention or their realisation in performance.

F is for Front-of-House and Finance. Staff in the front-of-house (a good old-fashioned category) now dispense 'Customer Care' (a modish piece of managerial cant which is, however, so all-pervasive that it has to be used and cannot be ignored). Customer care began with the ubiquitous American restaurant farewell greeting of 'Have a Nice Day' – or 'afternoon' or 'evening' or 'late evening'. We have all laughed at it. But we are all used to it. When BA check-in clerks (or do I mean desk officers) call me by my name as they give me an upgrade, I feel better: I am an individual passenger rather than just another customer. An impersonal process has become personalised: we may be part of a vast transport sausage machine but we can at least feel that we have our own skin. The arts are not there to provide mass experiences in commercially compressed and packaged forms. All the more important for us, therefore, to make our audiences feel personally welcomed even if they cannot be personally identified. I expect that customers care about customer care. Do centres show that they care about care?

F is also for Finance. Arts people are supposed to be 'no good at money'. Some are not. In my experience, good arts directors or administrators take it in their stride. Arts people are very good at cutting costs – all too often this involves accepting cuts in their own salaries. Arts folk are bad at looking after their own financial interests and none get rich on the process, except some stage directors and a handful of international musical performers who have undoubtedly earned their high fees. Most people work in the arts because they love them. Essentially, they subsidise the arts through their own low earnings. The canard that public funding of the arts provides comfy jobs at generous salaries – usually asserted by those who earn more in a day than the average arts employee does in a week – is a device with which to attack the whole idea of arts subsidy.

G is for Grants. No arts organisation – except Glyndebourne – can live without public grants. Too often the Glyndebourne model – through no fault of its own – is held up as one that others can or should follow. This is a delusion. It is a brilliant financial and artistic special case, a glorious one-off which has evolved over half a century, but has no implications for anyone else. Glyndebourne offers a very specific artistic programme for a specific audience at demanding prices in a carefully tailored environment and during a limited season. All the rest of us rely on grants of one sort or another from government or local government sources.

In the Barbican's case, the sole funder is the Corporation of London. Not content with funding the operations of the Centre, it also matches the Arts Council's grant to the Barbican's resident orchestra, the London Symphony Orchestra, and was until recently a very open-handed 'funder of last resort' to the Royal Shakespeare Company. These direct arts grants, and the additional sums the Corporation gives to academic institutions such as the City's conservatoire – the Guildhall School of Music and Drama – make it the third largest funder of the arts in Britain. Whether grants are a good or a bad thing, see 'Subsidy' below. As the recipient of a particularly generous one, it feels a good idea to me.

H is for Human Resources. Once upon a time we used to call it Personnel. That involved looking after people, but it did not sound sufficiently professional and managerially rigorous. 'Human Resources' all too often suggests that staff are no more than plant and can be as easily declared redundant. Remember, too, that once money turned into 'resources' – in another piece of managerial sleight of hand – there was less of it. So too with human resources: its main aim is to economise on them. HRT usually stands for Hormone Replacement Therapy. In improperly run institutions, HRT stands for 'human replacement theory'. Judge your HR team by whether they really behave like personnel managers.

I is for Ice Creams. Do not underestimate them. They earn money. Many people will buy an ice cream when they will not buy an interval drink, though some people are susceptible to a thick Belgian chocolate bar. Make sure these are part of your total retail offer. Price them correctly. Getting the price right could add a few thousand to your net income. There is a wider moral here: do not irritate your audience, who are not for the greater part well-heeled, by constantly edging up the overall cost of a pleasant evening out. Price sensitivity is not a piece of economics jargon; it means being sensitive about what you charge and not driving members of the public into shrieking, 'ouch, no thanks'. All prices for the supposedly minor items on offer at an arts event should be kept under constant review. When customer resistance is reached – say over the cost of a programme – the signs will be there for all to see. Be sensitive to it.

J is for Jazz. This is an important part of musical programming, a vital part of your programming mix. It can sell very well, at the right quality and in the right quantity. But do not think that jazz audiences are the same as those for pop or rock. Actually – as the broadcasters will tell you – jazz is a very minority taste, important historically but still only appreciated by a few. Presenting it is like adding a sharp spice to your venue: to be used lightly.

K is for Kitchens. They need constant attention on health-and-safety grounds. Nothing gives a venue a bad name so quickly as bad kitchens and – perish the thought – even an outbreak of food poisoning. Time and money spent on them is never wasted.

L is for Lavatories. Same as the above really. The state of the loos is taken by the public as a reliable indicator of the state of health of the institution as a whole. The music may be never so wonderful, the theatre never so sublime, the restaurants never so excellent – if the loos are not kept clean or if they smell, then most of the rest of your good work goes for nothing. I once told a newcomer to the arts management field that a large part of her job would be devoted to kitchens and loos. She thought I was either cynical or mad. A year later she confessed I was all too right.

M is for Marketing. This has become an art as well as a science. A good marketing team will know who the audience is, how they buy their tickets, at what prices, in what size of purchases, where they live and what socio-economic group they come from. They will tell you which ads or press articles brought in which sales. They will tell you who is likely to buy tickets for an event next time, on the basis of who bought them last time. They have a finger on the real pulse of your institution.

And yet. For my taste, it is a shade too mechanistic, too deterministic. While all of us as arts-goers have our preferred artists, our preferred events, I cannot be alone in wanting to be surprised, in wanting to be attracted to the unexpected, the unpredictable, the event that I would not normally go to and that the marketeers could not predict that I would. I have a dream of an audience made up of people who are swept in simply by enthusiasm for an event, not because they came to something like this a year ago. I want audiences of free agents, drawn magnetically by the prospect of quality, driven by free will and not hidebound by who they are, where they live or what they usually see. Marketing is essential – but it should be a guide not a determinant of your actions.

N is for Noise. Sound is good; noise is bad. Sound becomes noise when it is too loud or too intrusive for the person listening.

For instance, the sound of a band playing in the foyers of an arts centre – much advocated to encourage access and informality – becomes noise when it is too blaring or inappropriate for a significant number of others nearby. The sound of casual open-air performances around a centre and the buzz of the audience enjoying them becomes noise to local residents who may dislike the music or may simply dislike the idea of the existence of a centre at all. Monitoring the moment when sound becomes noise demands constant vigilance.

O is for Outreach. Is this the same as Education? Perhaps outreach includes education but goes wider in its attempt to involve the public in the activities of the institution. Outreach also implies a commitment to Access. And to Equality. Does it mean much left to itself? I doubt it but as you will hear the word used a lot then you should be aware of its existence as a portmanteau idea.

P is for Press and Programmes. Be nice to the press but remember that it is not the job of the press to be nice to you. Cultivate journalists by being as open as you can whenever you can. If you succeed, then you have increased the chance that they will trust you or give you the benefit of the doubt when things go wrong. Persuading the press to write feature articles in advance of an event, about a player or a performer, is worth thousands of pounds. As free advertising, it is an essential partner to your marketing strategy. It can persuade people that they should buy tickets. But a review is a review; nothing sells seats like a good one; nothing empties a hall like a group of bad ones.

By Programmes I mean the print the audience buys before entering the auditorium. They are an essential part of your public image. Think about the information you want to present about yourselves and what you do and what part the visitors can play in it. Audiences carry programmes home after the show, read them the following day, leave them lying around thereafter. They are part of your message to the public: here we are, come and join us. Do not let anyone else take control of one of your chief platforms for telling the public about yourselves. Try to make sure that they arrive on time for the show. Always make sure there are enough; running out of programmes leaves only irritated customers.

Q is for Quality. None of us can afford the very best performers providing the very best performances the whole time. But quality-control matters in another way. The audience senses inconsistency of quality. What you offer may not be the very best but it must be very good of its kind. Veering between high quality – when you can afford it – and lesser quality – when you can't – merely sells the audience short. They will notice. Equally, feeding the audiences a steady diet of the very good makes them less tolerant of the merely adequate.

R is for Resources – always insufficient and explained above – and Risk. The two have to be considered together but can never be balanced. Resources are knowable; the level of risk being run with a particular arts programme is notional. Resources are largely fixed; the risk could be limitless. The task is to reduce the risk to the point that it will not destroy the budget. But risk has to be taken or else you do not have an arts programme worth the name. If too little is ventured, then the institution is moribund and the audience will sense the deadly odour of playing safe. On balance, take more rather than less risk, but never shut your eyes to the amount of danger or the consequences of it all coming out on the downside. Be conscious of the financial failure but do not be driven by fear of it. Everyone finds comfort in a *succès d'estime*. Too many such 'successes' may break you.

S is for Sponsors. No organisation can survive without them. British bodies typically find a third of their funding from the public purse, national or local; a third from the takings at the box office; and a third from private, charitable or commercial sponsors. Do not expect sponsors to give money because they feel a duty to do so. 'Philanthropy' has no useful place in the dialogue with them. In the British model of taxation, there is no reason why it should.

They have to be led into a relationship where each side finds that a particular interest is served by co-operating. On the commercial side, such co-operation is frequently driven by the needs of marketing budgets. Arts organisations must be clear what they are providing in return for sponsorship and must be scrupulous and professional in delivering it.

T is for Tourists. We neglect cultural tourism, but it is a growing industry, a high-value industry, an industry that does not pollute the urban environment with coaches, coach fumes and junk-food litter. Stratford-upon-Avon and the Edinburgh Festival apart, the arts world has never co-operated actively and imaginatively among its own branches, never mind with the tourist boards, tour operators and airlines, to sell Britain's myriad cultural activities to foreign visitors. It is an opportunity waiting to be taken up, a great strategic opportunity for boosting sales and raising the image and standing of the arts.

U is for Utopia and the Unexpected. What is an arts utopia? One where everything outlined above has been addressed and realised at the highest possible level; one where the public funding is generous, predictable and proportionately supported by corporate and private sponsorship. A utopia is one where the organisers can offer a varied and balanced mixture of the known, the unknown and the unexpected and where the audience trusts the organisation so much that it takes the unexpected in its stride. Does such a utopia exist? Not that I know. Could it exist? Certainly, which is why the arts must continue to argue without shame or apology for support for what they do.

V is for Vision and Values. Arts organisations are intrinsically unlike business or industry because the commodity they deal with is absolutely unquantifiable. Of course, service and trust are also unquantifiable and lie at the core of many business activities. But then they are qualities that are an essential ingredient in a total measurable product. In the arts, values stand lonely and exposed at the heart of the activity. Without them, there is no activity. The vision expresses what they are. If you cannot imagine your vision, then express your vision in words, the values will never be understood or realised.

W is for the Wonder that, given all the obstacles and snares, any play is mounted, any concert is played at all, still more at the levels of quality that are achieved. Wonder is what you hope the audiences will feel at the end of a performance, when they contemplate the greatness of a work and the brilliance with which it was realised.

X is for Extending the audience's choice so that their experience of the arts is constantly refreshed and renewed, and the arts themselves do not slip back into the merely tried and trusted, which soon becomes the old and rejected.

Y is for Youth, the audience of the future. You must respect youth, accommodate it and learn from it. Do not appease youth, especially when it says that something is 'too boring', 'too difficult' or 'not relevant'. Much damage has been done to the arts, and to the young, by the educational system bending before these time-honoured reactions of the intellectually immature. You do no favour to the young by pretending that the arts are easier than they are or by adapting them to iron out the difficulties and at the same time removing the richness, the ambiguities and the complexity which are the only things that make the arts worthwhile.

Z is for Zing and Zip, the qualities that are needed in the arts to keep going through the alphabet of duties and responsibilities and obligations, the struggle for resources and sponsorship and access, and all the other letters of the arts alphabet.

If you can use all the letters of this alphabet in running an arts institution, then you have the ingredients for conducting a literate dialogue with your audience, your funders and yourselves.

Afterword: Art and Culture – Old Responsibilities, New Rhetoric?

I magine the Sea of Galilee. It is seven o'clock in the morning. The water is dead flat, bath-warm, dragonflies darting around at eye-level, the surrounding hills already shrouded in a September haze. The silence and the water are slightly parted by the genteel breaststrokes of British arts leaders. The occasional group stands chest deep musing over some mutual concern. Most do not. We take the soul-easing silence as a gift, a precious moment of preparation for the discussions to come. Make no mistake about it, a colloquium is shaped by its surroundings and this one was transformed by them.

I had expected to be entranced by the Sea and hills of Galilee. No one can be indifferent to the knowledge that these were the hills that Jesus and the Disciples walked, the waters that they fished, the villages where they met, taught, broke bread and began the prophesied journey to Jerusalem. But these are not 'heritage' tourist sites for the devout – though some are treated with more sensitivity than others – and they spoke to many of us in a way that was heart-catchingly quietening.

And it was not only the great Christian landmarks that cast their spell over us. The drive up the Golan Heights, the view from the top commanding the whole of Galilee, the knowledge that some of our Israeli co-locutors lost most of their best friends in the fighting, this too put our everyday thoughts into a deeper, contemporary perspective. For the physical setting of the discussions and the incredible wrenching of the imagination involved in moving across two millennia of history in a few hours played their essential part in making our discussions what they were.

The subject of the Anglo-Israeli Colloquium could not have been more fundamental, nor more appropriate as a topic for the closing thoughts in this book. 'Art and Culture – Whose Responsibility?' lays the question starkly before us. Unless someone accepts responsibility for art and culture, then their continued existence cannot be taken for granted. Israelis and Britons alike, we recognised a shared concern in our conversations, felt a common anguish, sought a mutual determination not to avoid the issue. If we did not find solutions, we felt that we at least indicated to ourselves some new ways ahead. I hope they offer the chance of escaping from some of the deadlocks within which we struggle in the everyday lives of the arts.

In most discussions about the arts and culture, still more so about the way they should be paid for, there is a reluctant consensus that the arts should exist in a healthy society. If such a consensus does exist, then it is only the start of the debate. The arts do not exist in a vacuum; they have to be willed into viable financial existence. Who does the willing? Who does the paying? Whose responsibility is it for the arts and culture to exist, better still to flourish? What are the respective roles of government, business, the people, and the arts themselves to create and sustain a vital artistic environment? That is what we discussed at Galilee.

Too often, these questions are answered – by arts people – using the 'should' form of the verb; thus the government, or business, or the voters 'should' fund the arts because the arts are useful and deserving and absolutely valuable in their own terms. While it is very easy to slip into a world of 'shoulds' and 'oughts', the fact is that such vocabulary impresses and persuades no one; these terms of implied obligation on the part of others butter absolutely no financial parsnips. The debate must take place without them.

Of course, the government has 'a' responsibility to foster the arts. This is not a sole or exclusive responsibility and it is heavily modified by practical questions about funding. If government is wise, it will shoulder that responsibility, for all the usually adduced reasons ranging from education, to tourism, to economic and urban regeneration, employment and even basic national self-respect. These are all the practical, mundane, contingent reasons for supporting art. This is government acting in a matter-of-fact, practical manner. But the trend to do it in partnership with others is growing and in keeping with the way we think about plural, decentralised societies today.

Audiences, too, have a real responsibility for keeping art and culture alive; without people, visitors, listeners and viewers, performances, events or exhibitions are dead. Business has a responsibility too, one that is imperfectly defined and inconsistently acknowledged. If arts and culture rely on this tripod of responsibility – state, people, business – it is a pretty unstable one, with each leg behaving as if it has a mind of its own, and often looking ungainly and precarious since each is of a different length and strength from the others. The idea of a 'shared' responsibility is over-ambitious. Even to say that each of these three elements has a responsibility is only to begin the discussion, not end it.

But there is another constituency whose responsibility for art and culture is often taken for granted or overlooked altogether – the broadcasters. Half a generation ago, the presence of the arts on the main terrestrial radio and television networks was palpable. The great landmark TV series of art were national events, part of a national dialogue, an expression of shared values and assumptions. Now arts programmes are peripheral, marginalised, weakened by the new laws of obligation to the marketplace. You would expect that of ITV. You would not expect it of the BBC, the second largest funder of the arts in Britain, and still the largest cultural influence in the nation. The BBC's new (self-imposed) market obligation is to maximise its audiences on all its networks at all times. This is a monstrous *trahison des clercs*, meaning as it does that programmes will not be judged on their intrinsic quality but rather on the size of the audiences they can deliver. The devastating impact of this attitude on the BBC's programming and thereafter on the national perception of and understanding about the arts is still being weighed and is yet to be fully felt.

The way the government looks at the arts is coloured and informed by the prevailing atmosphere in which we live – a post-modernist world where nothing is good or bad (only 'appropriate' or 'inappropriate' depending on circumstances), where everyone's opinion is as good as everyone else's, and value judgements have been relativised to the point of non-existence. There is no overriding political and social consensus on which a government can easily and comfortably base an arts policy. For politicians to assert that such a foundation exists demands a degree of confidence and reflects a wish to lead that the world of focus groups and media sensitivity renders unfashionable when it is not downright politically imprudent. Such confidence is increasingly rare in the prevailing atmosphere of millennial tension.

The world of those who work in the arts must play its part too. Increasingly, there is a robust readiness to stop defending the indefensible and to be ready to admit that some artistic activities are bad. Arts funders, even their peer groups, need to be ready to tell a wannabe dance company that they are not good enough to warrant funding as a full-time, independent dance group; or to tell an ethnic arts group that their work might be satisfying in an anthropological way, might have a certain local, social value, but fails by the artistic standards applied to others. Or to tell yet another would-be start-up symphony orchestra that London, for instance, has too many already. Picking winners in the arts may be a precarious business; but hanging on to losers becomes a bad habit.

While the business/commercial sector is now – in Britain – a significant funder of the arts, no one can say it 'should' perform that role. We have learned that companies have a weak sense of supporting the arts for reasons of pure 'philanthropy' – a word that is almost forbidden to use – and a strong sense of doing so for commercial, market-driven or PR reasons. We have come to accept, through long and perhaps bitter experience, that it is a waste of time approaching most companies with really risky or experimental artistic ventures. The answer to such proposals is all too often negative: 'Our clients would not be interested in seeing such and such.' In 1997, the English National Opera could find no one to sponsor their ambitious production of Zimmermann's *Die Soldaten*, admittedly not an ingratiating work but clearly an event of real artistic importance. If such conservatism, in the eyes of some, is a kind of commercially-driven censorship of artistic activity in everything but name, we take it as a fact of life. No one can be coerced into backing something they do not like.

For the arts do live in the marketplace, the challenging marketplace of public and private taste. They live with the disciplines and judgements of the box office, they face the verdicts and acclaim of criticism. Engaging business in funding the arts places them still more in arenas where purely arts-driven wishes are subjected to the scrutiny and evaluation of others with very different sets of values. Never before have the arts had to justify themselves and explain themselves more than they do today.

Where does this leave the responsibility of the people, to use an old-fashioned word – the audience, after all, is an altogether smaller subset of the larger group, the people, the voters, the public-at-large, call them what you will? Are the arts accountable to people – as distinct from audiences – in a democratic way? Where does democracy interpose itself in the relationship between the artist/performer and those who pay to watch and attend, or are taxed to enable the performance to take place?

In the general openness and candour generated by the spirit of Galilee, we admitted to a certain unease about the audience. 'We are afraid of audiences,' suggested one participant. 'We are afraid of giving things to people who do not know.' Why is this? Two immediate thoughts arise. Why do people not know about the arts? Or are we anxious about the length of time it would take to explain what needs explanation?

There was another observation: 'The audience wants more of what it knows and less of what it does not know.' Clearly, if this were true, there would be no way out along this road, one where everyone was condemned to a hellish eternity of recycling the familiar and avoiding anything that smacked of the different or the strange.

There was a way out of this creative and spiritual dead end, and we were drawn to it by looking closely at the particular experience of dance – not classical ballet, but modern dance. In Britain, with the creation of many new companies, an entirely new audience has emerged – one that is classless, often with a strong ethnic base, and one that is not afraid of modern music. This sudden burgeoning came about through clear policy direction from the Arts Council, and the strong creative leadership of some notably gifted individuals. This fortunate congruence of influences produced a consensus between creator, funder and audience, and one where – in one key comment – 'the success of these performers and performances did not depend on the communication of the whole.' What this meant was that you did not have to defend or advocate modern dance as a whole; you were simply invited to enjoy and admire a particular example of that art. But each particular success had the effect of advancing the cause of the whole. Each new company drove forward the form of contemporary dance by its own innovations. It did not have to make the case for the entire activity of dance and ballet as it did so. And yet the impact of a number of successful companies on a case-by-case basis created the awareness of and support for the entire genre of modern dance.

If that was true, the example of dance offered a case-study of the way in which artistic innovation and public consent could co-exist and march hand in hand. At the heart of this case-study lay the key experience of 'leadership'. What sort of leadership? Arts institutions must be more democratic, or at least more accountable (the idea of how this democracy works in this context still has to be teased out), but artistic creation – the responsibility to innovate, to renew, to develop – must lie with the performers and creators. This was not an arrogation of power, but represented an assumption of responsibility. After all, as one observer warned, 'the arts have nothing to do with democracy – but the arts have always been good at limiting tyranny.'

Four words summed up the rather solitary responsibility the arts have to shoulder, in the view of one participant: 'Leadership, reference, delivery and courage.'

If leadership and courage are called for, how brave are we in

shouldering our responsibilities to the arts? Brave in speaking up
and speaking out! 'Of course we have convictions,' said one
participant, and an event like this allowed us to air these
convictions, 'but we lack courage to speak out for those
convictions in the wider public domain.' Why is this? It struck
me that there are many reasons for failing to stand up for what
we believe in. Perhaps we are embarrassed by our acceptance of
public and business funding; we are challenged by the rhetoric,
vigour and practice of the market; we are too easily run ragged by
the arcane vocabulary and abstruse practices of management
consultants; we are wounded by charges of 'elitism' against which
we have no effective verbal counter; and when we do throw back
charges of 'philistinism', the charge of superiority and snobbish-
ness undoes us yet again.

We are fearful of rejection, deeply threatened by the indifference of the under-thirty-five generation, for whom culture equals
lifestyle and the behaviour and the outward symbols of fashion
and display; for whom the activities of the Internet, rock-and-
roll, drugs, films, TV and clubbing provide a feast of involvement
and engagement that we might call 'entertainment' but that they
know is 'culture' – their culture. How can we overcome such
indifference merely by speaking out against it? And the worst of
it is that they have stolen our word into the bargain. Instead of
culture defining the finest aspirations, the greatest achievements,
the best thoughts of society, it has been debased to a mere
description of how people live and behave, good, bad or
indifferent.

But the dialogue must start with the indifferent, the unknow-
ing, the agnostic, the unpersuaded, the downright hostile. The
dialogue must take place on terms defined by the arts world
because it is our existence that is under threat. First, by offering
our audiences a new deal, not a financial one but a new deal of
partnership. One colleague expressed it in this way: 'Give people
what they will like. But give them things they could not judge
beforehand.' This takes a little de-coding but I take it to mean
that the arts should want the audiences to like what they put on,
but the audiences should trust that what they may like in

practice is often not something that they could predict beforehand.

This idea of the extended hand of partnership went further:
'Help us to judge what goes on,' suggested one. I think that,
unconsciously perhaps, this phrase 'what goes on' includes a
double invitation – 'that which is taking place at an event' and
also 'that which is put on in the first place': in other words,
become a true partner in the activity. We did not believe that
market research could tell us what arts events to put on – but we
were looking ahead to a situation where the interaction with the
public was such that some sense of what the audience was ready
to take would become part of the artistic planning process. But
the audience had to play a more active part than that of a sheet
anchor slowing down the artistic drive of creativity and
innovation.

'But all this is too dreary,' objected one member. 'No one is
speaking about enjoyment.' He was immediately corrected.
'What the arts are offering is joy as well as enjoyment,' a more
complex idea. Another reminded us of the inscription over the
entrance to the Danish Royal Ballet – 'Not only for Pleasure'.

But we were dogged by a realisation that the old terms of the
artistic debate are no longer helpful. Old assumptions have been
passed by. As one participant said: 'In the past, there was a
consensus about the arts and culture that was summed up by the
saying: "However few it served, it helped the rest." ' We could no
longer rely on that as an assertion that could command
agreement, respect or funding. Many would – rightly or wrongly –
simply walk away from the idea as patronising and exclusive. So
we had to try and move ahead. The arts needed a 'new rhetoric
to express and enshrine old principles'. Perhaps it could be found
in the awareness that as intellectual disciplines change, reform
and alter their boundaries, as understanding of the world requires
an altogether new set of inter-disciplinary approaches, so the arts
would become an essential ingredient in understanding the vastly
changing world all around us and in explaining it. Far from being
marginalised and at the edges of contemporary understanding,

the arts would be seen as central in binding together a world otherwise destined for disintegration.

What words and phrases could be devised to shape and articulate this new rhetoric of justification for the arts? Here are some random key-phrases that emerged. The arts are about 'understanding the world'. Their most valuable function is 'taking people out of themselves', about 'seeing the other side of the mountain', about 'getting past the screen', as a way of 'making connections between people'. Some were grimmer: 'Ignorance is not much fun – and not much use either.' Perhaps the best was also the most affirmative, banishing elitism and embracing inclusiveness: 'The best for the best is the best for all.'

At Galilee, this group of people veered between optimism and pessimism, depression and excitement, realism and broad visions. My own conclusion is that in a tight corner, there is no room for pessimism, depression and realism. Such feelings will never get you out of it. A reaffirmation of principles must be a part of the new rhetoric, which itself needs to be founded on a new self-belief. An unqualified belief in excellence; a commitment to absolute standards; a deep caution about invasive relativism; and a sure sense that the sheer revelation and understanding that the arts have always offered and continue to provide will sooner rather than later persuade more than the already committed that Art Matters.